HOW TO BUY A HOME Without Getting Hammered

HOW TO BUY A HOME Without Getting Hammered

ONE OF AMERICA'S MOST RESPECTED HOME BUILDERS SHARES HIS SECRETS

David Weekley

with Patrick Byers

WORTHING BRIGHTON PRESS
P.O. Box 130746, Houston, TX 77219-0746
Voice: (713) 626-3330 Fax: (713) 626-2929
www.worthingbrighton.com

Library of Congress Cataloging-in-Publication Data

Weekley, David M.
How to Buy a Home Without Getting Hammered : one of America's most respected home builders shares his secrets / David M. Weekley. -- 1st ed.
p. cm.
Includes index.
ISBN: 1-885539-35-5

1. House buying--Handbooks, manuals, etc. 2. House construction. 3. Dwellings--Remodeling. I. Title.

TH4817.5.W44 2001 643'.12
QB101-200115

Second printing

Copy Editor: Virginia Galloway
Cover Design: Patrick Byers and Foster & Foster, Inc.
Book Design and Production: Foster & Foster, Inc.
Cover Illustration: Peter Pahl

For discount quantity purchases, please contact the publisher's special sales group.

For more information about the author, see: www.DavidWeekleyHomes.com

For more information about the publisher, see: www.WorthingBrighton.com

For more information about the book designer, see: www.fostercovers.com

WORTHING BRIGHTON PRESS
P.O. Box 130746, Houston, TX 77219-0746
Voice: (713) 626-3330 Fax: (713) 626-2929
www.worthingbrighton.com

This book is a result of working with and for thousands of wonderful individuals and families. We are each formed by the confluence of all of the experience and relationships in our lives; in that, I have been blessed beyond measure. Special thanks go out to the extraordinary Team at David Weekley Homes. We have worked, failed, learned, and succeeded side-by-side, customer by customer, over many years together. The realities contained herein have been brought to light through the experiences of those who work in the field daily. I am especially grateful to them for continuing to educate me on the ever-changing nature of the customer's desires and demands.

There are some individuals who deserve special recognition for their help. First of all, to Patrick Byers, whom I have worked with for over a decade and whose efforts have helped me put this work in readable form. To Michele Clements, who has shepherded this project from its inception and who has a deep understanding of our industry, our company and our customers. To Bob Rohde, a man with whom I've learned about floorplans and elevation designs.

In understanding that we are all products of our experiences, the most significant factor in my life has been my marriage to Bonnie, my high school sweetheart and soul mate. Her encouragement, understanding, and patience have made this book — and my career, for that matter — possible.

And to those considering a home purchase...this book is truly dedicated to you. You will never find the perfect home for the perfect price, yet not to take part in the joy and wholeness that home ownership can bring would be a grave mistake. To you I say, make a decision, move forward, put down roots and become a homeowner...there will never be a better time, than right now.

David Weekley

PREFACE

As someone who has dedicated over 25 years of his life to the art, craft, and business of homebuilding, I wanted to share some of what I have learned. Mine has been an education from the School of Hard Knocks, with some of the best teachers anyone could ask for. You might recognize some of their names: recessions, labor shortages, employee challenges, ever-changing buyer preferences, and 18% mortgage rates, to name a few.

If it is true that we learn from our mistakes, then you would find it difficult, if not impossible, to find a more learned man than I. During the last quarter century I have sold over 30,000 homes and, as you can imagine, I have made my share of mistakes. It is largely because of these mistakes that I feel compelled to write this book and help spare you unnecessary grief. The more we all know — buyers and sellers alike — about the business of homebuilding, the better it is for everyone.

America is fortunate to be the best-housed nation on earth, and I'm grateful to have played a part. Besides my experience as a homebuilder, I also bring 24 years as a husband and father of three to this endeavor. My family has moved into six different homes during that time — some used, some new, some large, some small, some we remodeled, and some we didn't. We've painted nurseries, laid linoleum, put up wallpaper and fences, and put in pools. You could say I've been totally consumed by this crazy business — and I've loved every minute of it.

It is my sincere hope that my personal experience, along with that of the 30,000 families who have put their faith in me over the years, will provide you with some nuggets of real value that will help you find the home of your dreams.

David Weekley

June 2001

CHAPTER ONE

Home Sweet Home

THERE IS NOTHING LIKE A HOME. I'M NOT JUST SAYING THAT because I've spent the last quarter century in the homebuilding business. There simply isn't anything else that comes close to the multi-faceted relationship we each have with our homes.

For our Cro-Magnon ancestors, home was a cave, a shelter to protect us from the elements and a sabre-toothed tiger or two. As we got better with tools, we learned to fashion sticks, straw and mud into our own "caves," free of the constraints of mountains and hills. Then came the wheel, and that led to moving vans, corporate relocation departments and Realtors®. OK, so I left out a few thousand years, but you didn't buy this book to learn about the history of architecture and construction.

This book is about the single biggest investment of your life — and how not to blow it. It is not about finding shelter. Sure, finding shelter is still somewhere on the list of reasons for buying a home, but it's nowhere near the top anymore. If you thought you were merely buying shelter, would you be willing to pay three years' salary for it? Would you even consider financing it for 30 years? If buying a home was still just about shelter, then we'd still be living in caves and I'd be a geologist, not a homebuilder.

With the possible exceptions of fine art, jewelry, and racehorses, a home may be the only thing that doesn't automatically depreciate in value after the sale. It's like nothing else we buy: not a television, not a computer, not an RV or a house boat.

Why is it, then, that so many Americans go into the largest transaction of their lives so ill-prepared? Too often, their only information comes from someone with a vested interest in the deal, like the builder, the Realtor®, or the mortgage company. Don't misunderstand me — most of these people are true professionals and strive to be unbiased and helpful. It's just that for something this huge, you should also have an independent, reliable source for home buying information. That's why I wrote this book.

No, home buying isn't just about shelter any more. It's about dreams and memories and friends and loved ones and family and status and self-esteem and belonging and how we see ourselves and how others see us. There really is nothing like a home.

CHAPTER TWO

It's Time to Do Your Homework

Look for your Homework Materials in the back of this book.

In spite of what you may have thought of it in school, homework is absolutely essential for successful home buying. As you read this book you will learn that nothing gives you a greater advantage during shopping for, buying, and building your home than doing your homework. Unlike your school days, there is no make-up exam here.

1. If you are a first-time buyer, are you ready to put down roots and a deposit?

This is a bigger commitment than a 12-month lease. Changing your mind six months after you purchase can cost you a lot more than a security deposit. You'll need to stay in one place long enough for your equity appreciation to cover closing costs, including title insurance, application fees, loan origination fees, attorneys' fees, etc. Depending on how the economy and housing market are doing, this could take two or three years, or even longer.

You also need to have a nest egg set aside. Down payments usually range from 5% to 20%, depending on the loan requirements determined by your credit rating and the mortgage company. (Often, if it's a government-backed loan like FHA, you can get by with as little as 3% down payment.) Then you have the closing costs, including the origination fee, survey fees, appraisal fees, insurance, attorneys' fees, title policy, taxes, and other miscellaneous fees. A 5% down payment on a $175,000 house is $8,750, plus approximately $5,000 in closing costs, bringing the total cash you'll need at closing to as much as $13,750.

Before you toss this book in the trash and start calling apartment locators, consider this: all that money you were paying in rent would now be going into the equity of your home. All the mortgage interest and property taxes are tax deductible. Still not convinced? A recent report from the Joint Center for Housing Studies at Harvard shows that 59% of homeowners with stock holdings still have more equity in their homes than in stocks. Let's look at a direct comparison of owning versus renting over five years.

We'll assume you're paying $1,295 per month in rent. If your landlord only increases your rent 5% per year, by the fifth year your monthly payments for rent would be $1,654.

Monthly payments on the $175,000 home will be in the neighborhood of $1,638 (at 7% interest rate with a 30-year fixed rate mortgage), including principal, interest, taxes, and insurance. Let's also assume you place the monthly "savings" between what you'd pay in rent versus a mortgage in an interest-bearing account earning 4%. If you're in the 28% income tax bracket, you'll save over $21,000 in federal income tax on the mortgage interest over the five years. If your home only appreciates a paltry 5% per year, it will be worth $224,588 after five years. Even after factoring in $1,500 in maintenance and $13,475 in Realtors'® fees and other selling costs, you will have paid $42,664 less to

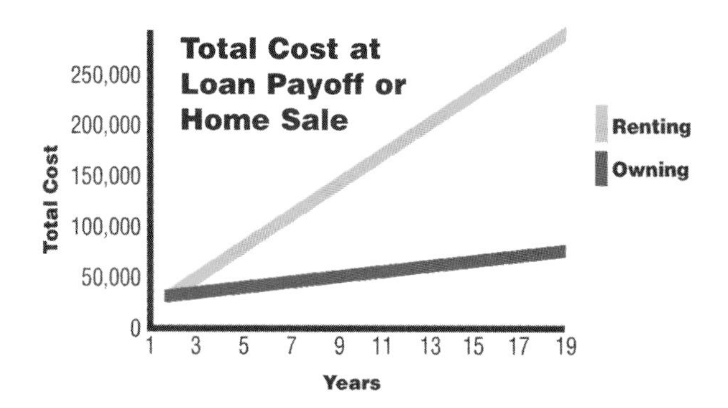

own than to rent in just five years. After ten years, you would have spent $116,504 less to own than to rent!

While it's true that the initial out-of-pocket costs for

purchasing are higher than a security deposit, it's false logic to say you can't afford to buy. The truth is, you can't afford to rent. If you don't have the cash yet, then start saving now. (Or borrow it from your favorite wealthy aunt.)

2. Where do you want to live?

If you have children, schools will probably be your first priority. If you aren't already familiar with the school district, ask around. Check with co-workers and friends. Are the schools conveniently located? Will the school bus pass near your home? Visit the schools during drop-off or pick-up times and talk to the parents. Tour the facilities.

Older neighborhoods are typically closer in than newer ones.

In some states you can also check standardized test scores to help compare students' academic level and the quality of teachers. Look at average class size and the student/teacher ratio. Review the breadth of school programs and extracurricular activities. Is the socio-economic environment a good fit for you and your children?

Consider the community itself. Do you prefer older neighborhoods? They're typically closer in with older neighbors and fewer children. Newer communities tend to be farther out with more neighborhood amenities. The families are often younger, with children.

Do you like a lot of trees or large open lawns? Are sidewalks important? Are there good deed restrictions that will protect the aesthetics and home values? The more bases you cover before you buy, the fewer unpleasant surprises you'll have later on when it might be too late.

Check the Homework Materials at the back of this book for "Rate the Neighborhoods", a neighborhood comparison chart that will help you narrow your search.

Compare your options carefully as you shop for your new home.

3. What do you want to live in?

We'll assume it's a house and not a trailer or a tent. Use the "House Hunting Wish List" in the Homework Materials at the back of this book to guide you through the process.

As you shop for your home, compare the available options to your "dream list" so you're aware of any compromises you might have to make. It's a lot to consider, but it has to be addressed sooner or later. Better to discuss it with your spouse in the privacy of your own home and come to a consensus rather than try to sort it out in front of an outsider who might not have your best interests at heart.

4. Have you tapped all your information sources?

There's a lot of research you can do that will help you fill in the blanks. Some of the best tools can be found in your home. If you have a newspaper, check the weekend home section and classifieds. If you're on the Internet you've got a world of knowledge at your fingertips, from Realtors'® and builders' web sites (I'm told davidweekleyhomes.com is a good one) to school districts, mortgage companies and payment calculators. Check out the

The Internet is an excellent source of information for home shoppers.

FannieMae site at www.homepath.com.

Don't forget to ask family members, friends, and co-workers. You'd be surprised how many people you see every day who have valuable experiences you can learn from.

Find a good Realtor® and you'll get a wealth of experience and information that will help you.

Check out city housing guides. They're like magazines with builder and developer ads and helpful maps and listings you can use to compare homes and communities.

5. Have you investigated the neighborhoods where you want to live?

As you begin shopping for your home, obviously you will be driving through the neighborhoods where you want to live, probably on a weekend. Be sure to visit the neighborhood on a weekday, too. Drive out early and join your future neighbors in their morning commute. Drive out after work and experience the evening rush hour first-hand. Is it something you can live with?

Spend some time on the weekends visiting with home-owners. Find out what they like best and what they like least. Could you be friends with these people? Will your children have neighbors close to their ages?

Are there grocery stores you like in the area? Is there a branch of your bank? A decent video rental store? What are the local tax rates?

Spend time in the neighborhoods to see if your family will fit in.

Then leave the neighborhood and check out adjacent neighborhoods. Are they improving or declining? What kind of businesses are nearby? Will any of the businesses bring unwanted traffic or noise?

There — that wasn't so tough, was it? Now that you've done your homework you can go out and play.

CHAPTER THREE

To Buy a New Home or a Resale?

YEARS AGO, A FRIEND OF MINE BOUGHT ONE OF THOSE "fixer-uppers" in a fashionable part of town popular with young professionals who wanted to live in the city. It was his first home and he was very proud. Shortly after closing, a Realtor® friend visited from out of town. "So, what do you think?" he eagerly asked. After a thoughtful moment she replied, "Do you know how to paint?" "Sure," he told her, picturing sunny weekends working with his wife. "Good. Paint a 'For Sale' sign and get rid of it as fast as you can."

Fortunately for my friend, this was the mid-seventies when home values were growing faster than those weeds in your garden. He satisfied his urge to remodel and made out OK.

Not everyone is cut out for buying a used home. Some people prefer them. If you're unsure of which group you're in, here are some questions that may help you decide.

- **Do you want to live close to the inner city?**
- **Are there no new homes available in the neighborhood where you want to live?**
- **Do you prefer the architectural style of an older home?**
- **Is it a really good investment opportunity?**
- **Are you mechanically inclined and enjoy working with your hands?**

If you answered "no" to the last question...

Did you recently invest in a high-flying stock pick?

Do you have a wealthy relative who really likes you?

There are times when buying "used" (or "pre-owned" as the used car folks are fond of saying) makes good sense. The most common reason comes back to the old real estate mantra: Location, location, location.

Often, if you're looking close in, your only choices are older homes in older neighborhoods. That's because cities grow much like the ripples created when you toss a stone in the water. It's not always concentric but it's always outward. The farther you get from downtown, the newer the homes. Occasionally you can find new construction in older neighborhoods, but — because of land values — these homes are often much more expensive than those in new home neighborhoods.

Older neighborhoods also usually mean older neighbors. Is that what you want? (Often, older neighbors spend more time at home and can keep an eye on the neighborhood.) If your kids are looking for others their age on the block, an older neighborhood may not be appropriate. These are important lifestyle decisions that can have a significant impact on your family's happiness.

Extras that come with a pre-owned home often include window treatments and landscaping. If they're well-done and you don't have to replace or improve them, this can represent a big savings over buying new where these items must usually be purchased.

Some older homes have classic architecture with broad appeal, but if they haven't already been updated, enlarging those kitchens and closets can make a new home seem like a bargain. While a handsome home in an older neighborhood could be a good investment, you should leave real estate speculation to the big boys with deep pockets. Your primary reason for choosing a home should be because you want to live there.

In some markets, depending on where you want to live, used homes can cost less than new ones. If your budget is limited, this may be an option, but beware. A used home can cost more to maintain, making it

If you aren't mechanically inclined, paying for repairs on a used home can become expensive.

penny-wise and pound-foolish. If you aren't mechanically inclined, paying plumbers and electricians to do all that work can add a lot to your housing budget. Used homes will also be less energy efficient, adding to your monthly utility bills.

Speaking of utilities, be sure to look for utility rights-of-way to see how they will impact your living. In addition, check out any deed restrictions that may limit where patios, fences, and other structures can be built. These restrictions might even dictate where you park and how you can utilize the outside spaces on your lot.

Clearly, maintenance is a prime concern for any home, new or used. A new home from a reputable builder is less likely to need repairs for the first few years, and if it does, your homeowner warranties and appliance manufacturers will most likely cover it.

Of course, if you don't particularly care about living in the city and you like the extra amenities that often come with planned communities, you might get more for your money with a new home. Many new communities have more active homeowner associations and enforce deed restrictions better, so you're less likely to have a bass boat parked in your neighbor's lawn. (If you're the one with the bass boat you'll want a neighborhood with no restrictions.)

If you buy a new home, you'll get a floor plan that will probably better fit the way your family lives. Older homes have more formal layouts, with smaller kitchens, baths, closets, and windows. New homes are more open with lots of windows, larger kitchens, baths and garages. You can also choose your wallpaper and other options, and you'll have all the latest modern conveniences. Then, years from now when the city has come to you, you can always paint your own 'For Sale' sign and start all over again.

New homes often have floor plans that better fit the way we live today.

Personally Speaking...

SAFETY MIGHT NOT BE THE FIRST THING YOU THINK OF when shopping for a home, especially if you don't have children or an older family member living with you. But life has a way of throwing us curves. Before you settle on a home, check out things like back yard fences and swimming pools — both in your yard and your neighbor's — and balusters (those little wooden posts that support the hand railing on balconies and stairs).

When my son Chris was five years old he fell from a second floor balcony. We were lucky. After spending the night in the hospital he came home with no serious injuries. (Although he claims his head still hurts today when he studies.)

Today's new building codes call for spacing between balusters to be no more than four inches. If you're buying an older home, be doubly careful.

CHAPTER FOUR

The Ten Biggest Mistakes in Home Buying

1 Not doing your homework

You've probably heard the old maxim: "Knowledge is power." Nowhere is this truer than in real estate. With a price tag that's two or three times our annual salary, if ever a purchase demanded preparation it is home buying.

Do your homework before you start shopping for a home.

It can be overwhelming when you think about all the factors that can affect a home's value: its location, the school district, deed restrictions, taxes, amenities. That's why it's imperative that you do your homework before you start. With all of the information available today on the Internet, from Realtors, and in housing guides, there's really no excuse for entering the market ill-prepared (see chapter 2).

2 Trying to make a shrewd investment

It's easy to think we are all financial geniuses. No doubt some of you are. So, Mr. Gates and Mr. Buffet, you have my permission to move on to the third biggest mistake in

home buying. As for the rest of you, forget everything they told you in that late-night infomercial. While real estate investing can make a great career, it's no place for amateurs.

As simple as it may sound, when it comes to buying a home, your best bet is to choose one that appeals to you. The chances are very good that if you like it others will, too.

Am I suggesting that you throw caution to the wind? Lead with your heart and not your head? Absolutely not, but if you choose a neighborhood where you and others like you want to live and a home that's attractive and structurally sound, then you probably won't go wrong. If you want to be known as a shrewd real estate investor, then wait at least three to five years before selling and you can tell everybody that you outguessed the market.

3 Choosing a poor location

OK — you've found the perfect home. It's in a good school district, it's got great curb appeal, a terrific floor plan that fits your family and the price is right. The only drawback is the bowling alley that backs up to it. Walk away.

Nothing spoils life and resale value like a poor location.

If it bothers you now, don't think you will learn to live with it. The flood lights from that office building across the way will only get brighter with time. The planes on final approach to the airport will only get louder and more frequent.

As a rule of thumb, stay away from busy streets, railroad tracks, airports, shopping centers, halfway houses, barking dogs, and beekeepers.

The best looking home, the most extravagant landscaping, tall fences, and insulated windows will never overcome a home site near a pig farm (No offense to pig farmers).

4 Overlooking an inferior floor plan for an attractive exterior

I don't mean to downplay the importance of curb appeal. A home that turns your head as you drive down the street can be a real asset. Resale will be a lot easier if you don't have to stand on the curb shouting, "No, wait! I know it looks bad, but this home's got great personality!" If the romance doesn't continue when you open the door, then you've got a problem that will be difficult to unload.

You want a home that makes your heart beat faster

when you first open the door. It's got to have a layout that makes people feel comfortable, one that responds to the way we live today. Open. Friendly. Functional.

I've seen it happen a hundred times. Buyers approach a home with an exterior they're not crazy about, then they discover a fantastic floor plan, and when they come back out, the exterior seems to have magically improved.

If I had to choose between a good-looking exterior or a knockout interior — and I couldn't have both — I'd choose the great interior every time. After all, that's where you live every day.

5 Not considering how your family wants to live

We all carry around a mental picture of the perfect home. If you're a child of the 60's your ideal home probably looks like the Cleavers' house. Younger shoppers may be searching for the Bradys' or the Cosbys' home. These images seldom fit the way we really live.

It's also not about finding a home your parents would like (unless they're helping with the down payment). It's not choosing a home your best friends would want.

This home only needs to fit one family — yours. Your

comfort and happiness depends on how well you can judge that fit.

Start by thinking of how you live now. Try not to be influenced by those fantasies of how life would be if only you had the right home. If your idea of fun is watching reruns of Jeopardy in your pajamas, then look for a TV room that accommodates your favorite naugahyde reclining lounger. If you like to have friends and family over for informal get-togethers, then look for a large kitchen that's open to the family room. How many rooms do you need? How should they be arranged? Master up or down? Will you have a use for a home office?

Don't overlook how your family lives outside, as well. Will you use a pool or would a hot tub suffice? Do you like to garden and work in the yard, or would you rather have less maintenance?

When judging a home, don't overlook how your family lives outside, as well as inside.

If you're buying a used home, you'll have to look

beyond the current owner's décor and furnishings. If it's a builder's furnished, new model home, the toughest part will be facing the fact that the decorator and furniture don't come with it. If you're honest with yourself, you can find a home that will fit your family and feel like...well, home.

6 If buying a resale, not having the home properly inspected

I can't emphasize this one enough. When you find your dream home, it's love at first sight. As with all love affairs, you begin to lose your objectivity and see only what you want to see. "OK, so the foundation is cracked. But, Bif, isn't this the cutest little window you've ever seen?" Now is a good time to seek professional help.

They're called structural and mechanical inspectors. Good ones are worth every penny you pay them. A good one is licensed by the state (ask to see his or her certificate) and has no personal relationship with you, the seller, or the Realtor. This is someone you pay for a professional, unbiased opinion about the structural integrity and mechanical performance of the home you're planning to buy. They will inspect every major component of the house from the foundation to the rafters, including the central air, furnace, water heaters, plumbing, and electrical. You will also want to have the home inspected for termites. As much as it may hurt to hear something negative about the one you love, this is when you want all the ugly truth.

You and the seller will be given a written report with a list of items that must be repaired before you close the deal. Usually the contract spells out limits on what the seller is obligated to pay for repairs. If the cost of recommended repairs exceeds this amount and the seller is unwilling to pay for them or to adjust the sales price, DO NOT proceed. (You may elect to pay the difference if the overall deal is still a good one.) This could be the toughest decision of your life, but ignore the engineer's warning and you will live to regret it.

7 If buying new, failing to check out the builder's reputation

If you're shopping for a new home, you probably know where you want to live, so you'll be comparing homebuilders in that area of town. You'll look for home designs that appeal to you in a price range you can

afford. Once you've narrowed your search to one or more builders' homes, your next step should be to take a long hard look at the builders. Here are the most important questions you should answer about any builder before you let them build your home:

- **How long have they been in business?**
- **How many homes have they sold?**
- **What do their homeowners think of them?**
- **How many of the homeowners would buy from the builder again?**
- **What do other builders say about them?**
- **What industry recognition have they received?**
- **What does the Realtor community think of them?**
- **What kind of warranties do they offer?**
- **Do they have a department solely dedicated to warranty issues?**

The best way to check out a builder is to ring some doorbells and knock on doors. Visit the neighborhoods where they build and ask the homeowners about their experiences. You should talk to at least three to five neighbors and get a consensus before you make one of the largest investments of your life.

If you don't get satisfactory answers to most of these questions, choose another builder. If none of them pass this test, choose another part of town. Beyond all the fancy advertising and hype, builders have only one thing of real value: their reputation. If the one you're considering doesn't have a good one, they shouldn't get your business.

8 Not getting what you want because you're impatient

To borrow a phrase from the Rolling Stones, time is on your side. Show me someone in a hurry to buy and I'll show you someone who pays too much. There are a lot of things you can rush into and recover from later, but this does not include marriage or buying a home. Never, ever, ever, rush into buying a home. Have I made my point yet? It is the single largest investment most of us ever make. It requires an enormous amount of energy, effort, and research. It takes time to do it right.

You need time to do your homework. You've got schools to check, tax rates to compare, mortgage companies to shop, neighborhoods to drive, and — if it's a new home —

you need to check the builders' reputations (See #7 above).

If it's a used home, you need time to negotiate. Seldom should you pay the "asking price" on a used home. The longer you can take, the better the deal you can usually make. If you find yourself in an unavoidable time bind because of a transfer or the impending sale of your home, try to make arrangements to delay the purchase. You can always store your non-essential things and rent in the interim. Sometimes people who purchase your home are willing to lease it back to you on a pro-rated basis if you need extra time. It doesn't hurt to ask and it could save a lot. Do the math. If patience can save you $5,000 on the purchase price, wouldn't that be worth it?

Whatever you do, even if you don't have time and you must move forward, try not to show it until after the price is set.

9 Waiting for a better time to buy based on the market and interest rates

Buy low. Sell high. It's a great plan if you're a fortuneteller, but for the rest of us mere mortals, here is the best advice for when to buy a home: There is no time like the present. You know what houses cost. You know what interest rates are. You know you have a job (If not and you're not independently wealthy, maybe you should consider putting it off).

Warren Buffet says, "the rear view mirror is always clearer than the windshield." Looking back, we all can see when the best time to buy a home would have been — although at this writing, it would be hard to find a better time than now, with reasonable interest rates, low unemployment, and an expanding economy. Who can predict the future? The best we can do is learn from the past. History shows that those who purchased homes and kept them for three to five years or more did better than those who didn't. How can you argue with that?

Those who purchase homes and keep them for three to five years do better than those who don't.

Will interest rates be lower some day? Probably — then you can refinance. Will home prices ever be significantly lower? Probably not. Will you be making more money in the future? We all hope so. Do you have a crystal ball? Stop your waiting. Just do it.

10 And the biggest home buying mistake... drum roll, please...not buying at all

No place to call your own. No control. No tax break. No appreciation. No equity. No kidding.

CHAPTER FIVE

The Secrets of Good Design

What gives a home curb appeal?

THIS STORY WAS REPORTED IN THE LOCAL NEWSPAPER. A man showed up at the police station, lost. While visiting his daughter from out of town he had taken a walk and couldn't find his way home. No, he wasn't senile. He was in Levittown, New York, where all the homes and all the streets looked exactly alike. In the 1950's, Levittown was a shining example of American ingenuity.

Seeing the need for affordable housing after World War II, William Levit borrowed an idea from Henry Ford and satisfied that demand on a potato field outside New York City. Since he couldn't put the houses on a conveyor belt he decided to put the workers on one. Carpenters, electricians, plumbers, painters, and roofers followed each other down the street building the same house over and over, street after street, block after block. It was the original cookie cutter community, totally devoid of any curb appeal. Fortunately, things have changed.

Have you ever been driving through an attractive neighborhood when, suddenly, one home just reaches out and grabs you? It's what Realtors® call curb appeal. As the term implies, curb appeal is the attractiveness of a home viewed from the street or the curb. It's your first impression. It's the cover by which you've been told you can't judge the book. Some homes have it. Some don't. Here's how to make sure the one you buy does.

Curb appeal is your first impression of a home from the street.

Start with trees. Nothing adds as much to the allure of a neighborhood as trees. If you're looking in a new community built on a rice paddy or potato field, check out the tree budget of their landscaping plan. If you don't see a substantial number of newly-planted trees, then you're barking up the wrong one. There are species of trees that grow fast and can change the look and feel of a neighborhood. If you're planning on living there a while and are patient, you could see the value of your home grow as quickly as the trees.

Also look for streets that have been laid out aesthetically with curves and cul de sacs. They give a much better feel than straight streets and square corners. So do

large setbacks, the distance from the curb to the home.

The better neighborhoods offer a variety of architectural designs that complement each other.

The neighborhood should have a good variety of architectural designs. You don't want to see the same elevation — that's a builder's term for the "front" of the home — every fourth house. What about exterior finishes? Is there a blend of brick, siding, stone, stucco, etc.? A pleasing mixture of 1-story, 1-1/2-story, and 2-story designs adds character to a neighborhood. What size are the lots? Is there a comfortable distance between homes?

Garages can have a huge impact on a neighborhood's curb appeal. Front-load garages face the street and can expose a lot of clutter. Side-loads and rear-loads require larger lots and are usually more expensive. So are detached garages with covered walkways. Are there deed restrictions that prevent aluminum carports from springing up? What kind of fencing is allowed?

All of these seemingly unrelated items can have an

effect on your home's curb appeal and future resale value.

Now let's look at the home itself. During the 80's and early 90's there was a trend in new construction in many areas that called for massive red brick homes and large entries with windows revealing chandeliers and winding staircases. These days, people seem to prefer more neighborly elevations. (I'm happy to see that porches and comfortable facades with siding are making a comeback.)

What architects call massing and proportion contribute as much to curb appeal as anything. Do the windows fit the mass? While they shouldn't be too small, they shouldn't overpower the home, either. Are the dormers properly proportioned or do they look like afterthoughts? Do the porch columns look sturdy or are they too thin? Look at the roofline: Is it varied with interesting angles and an attractive pitch or is it too flat and featureless?

Massing and proportion are important ingredients in a home's curb appeal.

Does the landscaping complement the

architectural design? Trees and shrubs should frame the home, not hide it. There should be flowerbeds that add seasonal color to make the home distinctive.

As you can see, it's not just one thing that gives a home curb appeal. It's the whole package: neighborhood, a variety of exteriors, interesting rooflines, and attractive landscaping. The home you choose may not have all the ingredients, but the more it has, the more valuable it will be.

Notes

CHAPTER SIX

Reading Between the Lines

Uncovering a floor plan's hidden value

TO SOMEONE UNACCUSTOMED TO THEM, DECIPHERING blueprints can be like reading the Dead Sea Scrolls, but the floor plan is our friend. It tells us almost as much as a walk-through of the completed home. Also, it's a lot cheaper to make changes to a floor plan. You just need to know what to look for and what to avoid.

Actually, the term floor plan is misleading and may explain why the general public so often misunderstands them. Taken literally, floor plan implies only two dimensions with a focus on the floor, but most of us spend our time a good five feet above the floor. A better name would be space plan or flow plan or living plan. An informed eye can find far more information on the average floor plan than the layout of the floor. Things like sight lines, room adjacencies, traffic patterns, window and door placement, arches and columns, and room volume can tell you how a home will look and, more importantly, how it will live.

Top Trends in Home Design

The world seems to be changing faster than ever today. Think back to life before the personal computer, e-mail, faxes, cell phones, and beepers. It hasn't been that long ago. No wonder home design is a moving target. In your hunt for a new home the trick is to set your sights somewhere between functionality and resale. (No matter how cozy that home office might be, if it isn't wired for broadband modems with space for faxes, scanners, and printers it's just another bedroom in disguise.)

Trends are not fads. This is not about shag carpeting and lava lamps. These are genuine responses to fundamental shifts in how we live. Look for the following features in any home you consider.

Flexibility

Secondary rooms need to fulfill more than one specialized need. Think of a nursery that can become a sitting room, or a bedroom that, with an attached bathroom, can become a mother-in-law suite.

More Garage Space

The SUVs are taking over. People are driving larger and larger vehicles and owning more of them. Today's garages must handle these behemoths and all that other "stuff" you don't want cluttering your house.

One Big Living Area

Formals are for prom night. People would often rather

have a bigger family room with specialty spaces for reading or watching TV than a formal living room.

Computer Friendly

This doesn't just mean plenty of electrical outlets. There needs to be space for computers and peripherals in the study, the master bedroom sitting area, and the kids' rooms.

TV Living

News flash: the battle between the TV and the fireplace for room dominance is over. TV won. DVD, satellite dishes, and surround sound have made our TVs indispensable. Accommodating them is a priority.

Home Office

This is no longer a fantasy. More Americans are working from home than ever before. Part-time and full-time telecommuting will continue to grow and should be anticipated.

Bonus Rooms

It's that space above the garage or family room. It's the attic area under that high-pitched roof. Bonus rooms are those spaces you can count on growing into in the future. The more the merrier.

Personally Speaking...

YOU MIGHT BE SURPRISED when you see which part of the home your family uses most. Sometimes the "living" room is not the living room. When my kids were younger, a lot of our time was spent in the master bath. Often Bonnie and I would spend half an hour in there getting ready while our toddlers would entertain the dog playing dress-up in mommy's shoes and daddy's ties.

As our family got older, our "living" room became the kitchen/breakfast/family area. (That's right. The home we live in is very much like the ones we design, because it works!) While Bonnie makes dinner in the kitchen, James and Chris are doing homework at the dining table. 16-year-old Robin is on the phone and I'm reading the paper in my lounger. We're all busy doing different things — together, within audio/visual contact. It's how today's busy families stay close.

Multi-functional Kitchens

This is the "heart" of the home. It's "command central." The kitchen today functions as an entertainment zone, a conference room, and fast food take-out, as well as a place to prepare the occasional meal. It must be convenient for one cook, yet be spacious enough for a holiday gathering.

Casual Exteriors

Home elevations (exteriors) are less forbidding and more inviting. The emphasis today is on living outside the home as well as inside. Front porches give us a place to sip cold drinks and watch the world go by. They also help with energy consumption by shading windows.

Sight Lines: why they're more important than square feet

Two homes have the same square footage yet one seems much larger than the other does. How can that be? No, it's not smoke and mirrors — it's because of sight lines. Sight lines are what you see from any given point in the home, whether you're standing in a doorway or seated in a room. When sight lines are obstructed by a wall or a door the home will feel smaller. Open things up with a hint of what lies beyond; add a strategically placed window and the home will always look and live larger.

People talk about "the good old days." But the "good old days" weren't all that good for the average homeowner during the 50's and 60's (unless he happened to be a bear who liked living in caves).

The typical non-custom home built before 1980 was an unimaginative combination of small, boxy rooms, dark hallways, and tunnel-like stairways. Front doors often opened to small entries that felt more like solitary confinement than "welcome to my home."

It wasn't really the builders' fault (you'd expect that from me, wouldn't you). It's just human nature. People have always wanted more for their money, so builders gave them more rooms. Houses were often described in terms of how many rooms they had: "Mr. Gatsby? Oh yes, he's the chap who lives in that 40-room swankienda up on the hill." Builders figured that if people are into counting rooms, then by golly they'd close off as many spaces as they could and start counting! Remember swinging doors that separated dining rooms from kitchens? Compared to today's open concept designs, the homes of the good old

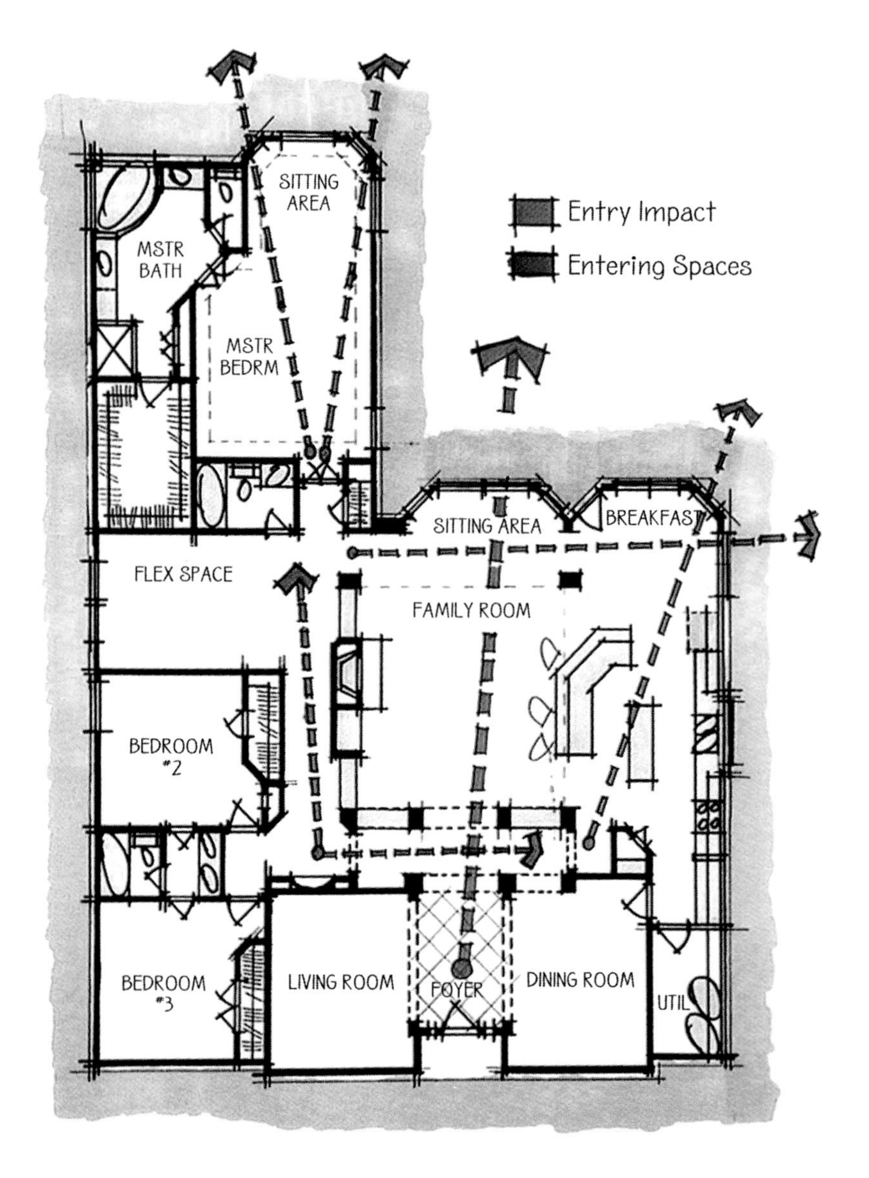

FIGURE 1 Sight lines are the key to making a home "live" larger. In this example, one can stand in the foyer and see the living room, dining room, family room, and beyond, through windows at the rear of the home.

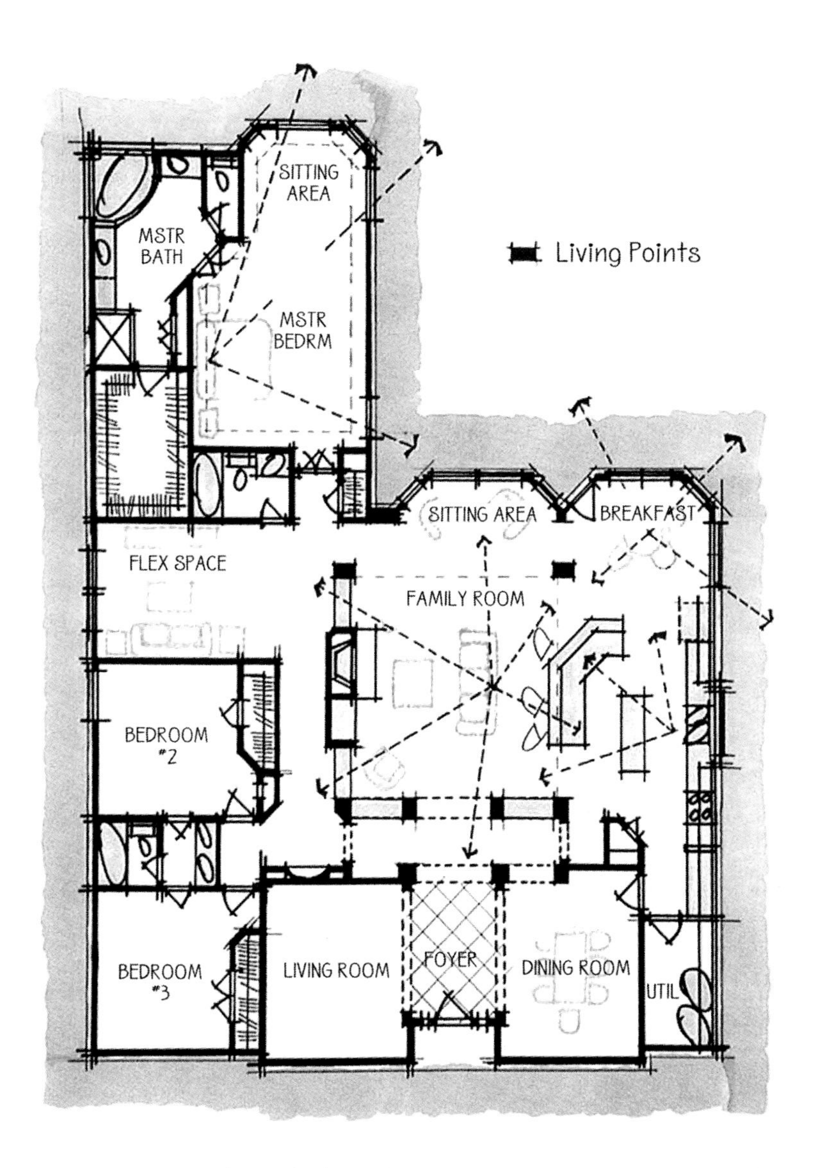

FIGURE 2 Notice the sight lines from various sitting positions in the home. From the family room sofa one can see the foyer, dining room, kitchen, and backyard. There are multiple sight lines from the kitchen — even the master bedroom provides views of the courtyard.

days were claustrophobia waiting to happen.

We live more openly today than we did 25 years ago. Our lives are busier and our schedules are fuller. In between work, school, soccer practice, karate lessons, Scouts, Tae-Bo and the chiropractor we're looking for more time together. Open homes encourage that togetherness and keep us in touch.

Open floor plans encourage togetherness.

Today the best-designed homes always take into consideration what people see when they open the door, and not just the front door. A bedroom with the door to one side of the room will seem larger and make it easier to place your furniture than if the door is in the middle of the wall.

Checking a home's sight lines can be a lot of fun. All you need are house plans, a ruler, and a pencil. Start from the middle of any doorway or opening and draw a straight line to various focal points in the home. Does the line stop in that room or does it pass through several?

Does it intersect a featureless wall or will you get a glimpse of a fireplace or a window and the courtyard beyond?

Once you've mastered the technique of judging doorway sight lines, you're ready to move on to Sight Lines 202: testing sight lines from various sitting positions in the home. What will you see from the breakfast table? The family room sofa? From your bed as you read the Sunday papers?

As you move through a home, it's far more interesting to get a preview of what's to come with subtle hints and intriguing clues of the spaces beyond than to be cut off from the rest of the home.

Rules of Room Placement: we all need our space

Do you really want your children's bedrooms directly over the master bedroom? I can give you all kinds of reasons why that's not a good idea. We all love our children, but there are times when even the closest of families need their privacy. The best plans keep the master at a comfortable distance from other activities in the home.

Not all adjacency issues deal with privacy; sometimes

it's about togetherness. For example, kitchens should not isolate the person preparing the meal (although if you cook like I do, sometimes hiding what goes on in the kitchen can be a good thing.) Most of the time large, eat-in kitchens are great places to bring families and friends together. By combining food preparation and dining we create wonderful opportunities for conversation and closeness.

The game room concept is changing, too. Instead of just converting an unused bedroom, families are finding children's retreats to be far more useful. A children's retreat consists of a common recreation/study area that serves as the hub of the children's activities and is surrounded by the bedrooms. This area of the home becomes a special place just for the kids, where they can do their homework, play games or watch TV while mom and dad enjoy some quiet time with a movie or reading by the family room fireplace.

Children's retreats are becoming more popular today.

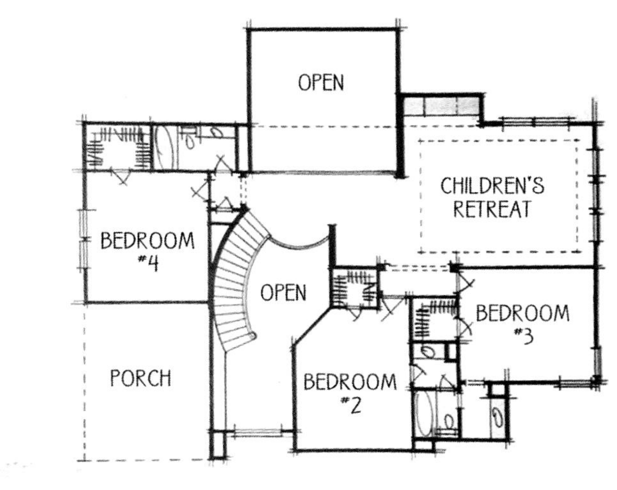

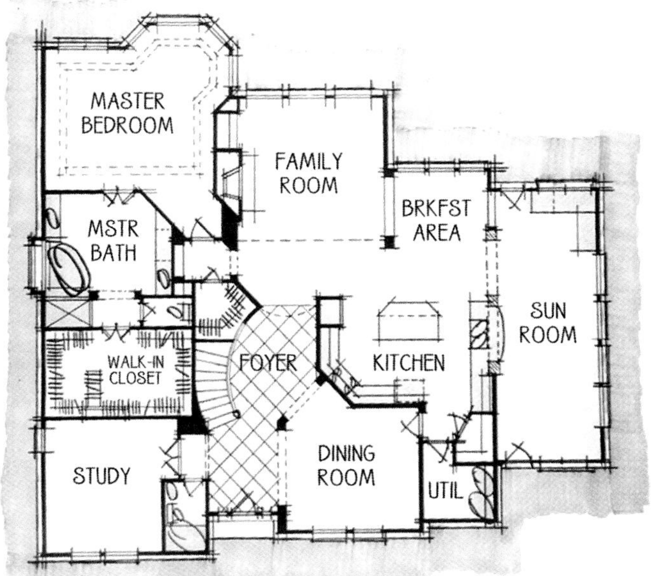

FIGURE 3 Room placement plays a large role in how "comfortable" a home is. Above, the master bedroom and bath are given their own wing, away from the hustle and bustle of the rest of the home. No other room is placed above the master sleeping area for added privacy. Upstairs, a "children's retreat" forms the hub of the other bedrooms.

Directing Traffic: how we move from room to room

In the not-too-distant future, floor plans will be animated. They'll show you sight lines, light sources (both artificial and natural from windows and skylights), room-to-room sound transmission, relative air temperature, and traffic patterns. That's when homebuyers will clearly see that a floor plan is not about how the home looks when you're standing still or seated. The success of a floor plan is how you move through it.

These days, we rarely use hallways to move from one space to another. They waste space and they're dreary. Now we use other rooms as our passageways. This has the added advantage of making small space rooms seem larger when they are open to other rooms with good sight lines. When you walk from the master bedroom to the kitchen, though, do you want to walk between the sofa and the TV? If your master bedroom is upstairs, do you want to walk down the stairs and pass through the entry in your pj's to get a glass of water? Try to visualize coming home with your arms full of groceries, making your way from the garage to the kitchen or pantry.

The best floor plans use a technique called horizontal

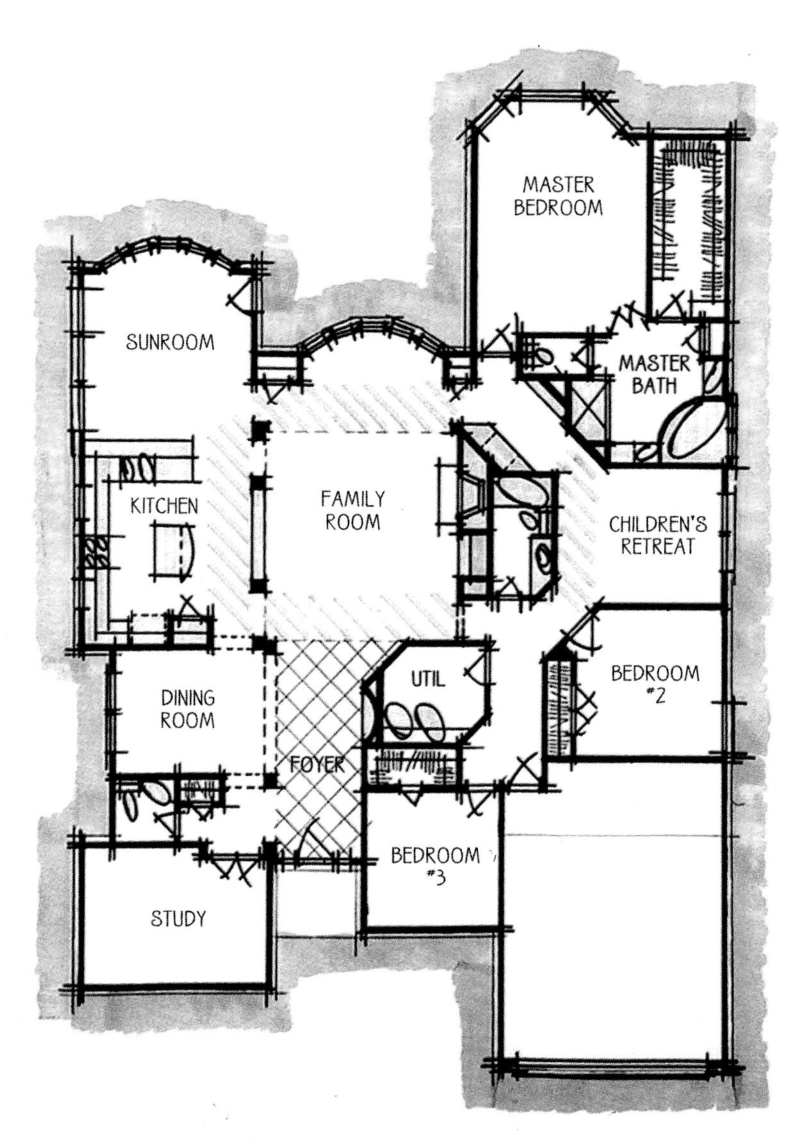

FIGURE 4 Horizontal banding provides traffic flow that doesn't interfere with the primary use of the room. In this example, passage from the master bedroom, children's retreat, and second bedroom to the kitchen has been designed into traffic areas around the family room, keeping you from having to walk through the middle of the room.

banding to accommodate traffic patterns. Look at the floor plan in figure #4. The family room is located between the kitchen on the left of the home and the master bedroom, children's retreat and second bedroom to the right. In this example, two traffic areas have been designed into the space for better circulation. Horizontal banding avoids a traffic pattern that would force you to navigate diagonally through the family room and keeps you from tripping over furniture.

A poor floor plan also creates a nightmare for furniture placement. "Yeah, that would be a great place for the sectional, only we'd have to hurdle it to get through the room."

Unless you've named your home Tara and are waiting for Rhett to return, having a stairway open into the entry is not always practical. A staircase should be positioned where it ties into the natural circulation of the home and makes sense. For example, it's sometimes a better idea to have it come to the family room or kitchen toward the center of the home for better access and a better use of space.

Also, don't settle for just one way into the kitchen. This is the heart of the home. The more ways in, the merrier. You don't want bottlenecks during parties and family gatherings. A good rule of thumb is three ways in, minimum. Five is even better.

Windows and columns and stairs, oh my!

It doesn't take a lot of windows to make an impact on the personality of a home. You just need to know where to put them. As you may have guessed, sight lines play a large role here, too.

An expansive rear wall in the family room doesn't have to be filled with two-story windows to bring in the beauty of a landscaped backyard. Even if the ceiling is vaulted to twenty feet at the wall, you don't need windows all the way to the top. Besides wasting a lot of energy, the windows might not improve the look and feel of the room. A strategically-placed set of six or eight-foot windows can have just as much impact and be more economical.

Sometimes small windows under cabinets can have a huge influence on the "feel" of a kitchen. A bow bay window in a small dining area will make it seem much larger.

Pay special attention to the interior/exterior relationship created with windows. What direction does the window face? Will it give morning or afternoon light? You might want eastern exposure for a breakfast room window that frames colorful landscaping bathed in morning light. Large windows with western exposure may not be a good idea for a family room with a large screen TV. A clear glass window over the whirlpool tub provides great views for you; unfortunately, the same is true for your neighbors if the window happens to be oriented to the side of the home.

Windows determine the interior/exterior relationship in your home.

Fancy "eyebrow" and Palladian windows can add character to any home. They also add to the cost, so be sure they are located where they will have the greatest impact and not hidden away where people can't enjoy them every day.

One of the best ways to define spaces and rooms where privacy is not an issue is with columns. They keep sight lines open, allow for better flow, and maintain important relationships between rooms that function together, like the kitchen and dining room.

For example, a series of arched columns can separate

the kitchen from the family room without separating the cook from the action. A column in an open family room, placed just right, can help define the traffic pattern from the master bedroom to the kitchen. Pay close attention to scale when judging columns and arch thickness. In general, the larger the space, the thicker the column or ending wall should be. For best effect, don't settle for anything less than eight inches in width, and preferably a foot.

Often the best way to define space is with columns, instead of walls.

Space, The Final Frontier: living room vs. storage room

Sooner or later, the single biggest issue in any home's layout becomes *How much am I willing to pay for storage?* If money were no object, our pantries would be the size of Winnebagos and our closets would feel like Carnegie Hall, but in the real world, where most of us live, trade-offs must be made. It usually sinks in when we tell the builder, "Oh, there's no way I can live with a closet that small!" "Fine," he says, "How many square feet should we take from the kitchen to make your closet larger? Or should it come from the family room?" It's not an easy call.

Before you start chopping or settling, ask yourself if there are any untapped storage opportunities. Do you have access to the area under the stairs? Have you asked for flooring in the attic? Is your central air equipment tucked neatly to the side of the attic space? What about the space above the garage? Can that water heater go in the attic, too? Do all closets have two or three tiers of rods and shelves on each wall? Is there room for another shelf up near the ceiling in that pantry? Is it time for a garage sale?

Have you used the storage space that's available under stairs?

Only after you've exhausted these possibilities should you tackle the ugly task of sacrificing living space for storage space. Remember Weekley's Law: no matter how much stor-

age space you design into the home, it will never be enough. Don't be too hard on yourself. Scientists may soon discover that our species is more closely related to the pack rat than we ever imagined.

Good Plan/Bad Plan

Remember those magazines in the dentist's office when you were a child, the ones that had pictures with hidden objects you had to find? Comparing floor plans is almost as much fun, except if you miss things here, you don't get to leave your mistakes in the magazine rack at the dentist's office. You have to live with them every day.

Take your time when comparing floor plans and use the techniques in this chapter to read between the lines. The more mistakes you find at this stage, the fewer you have to pay for later.

Practice what you've learned with the following comparison. At the end of this chapter are two floor plans that, at first glance, seem quite similar — same type of plan, same square footage, same basic room relationships. Take a closer look, though, and you begin to see some important differences.

Let's start in the foyer. Which entry would you prefer:

Plan A with one sight line to the rear window of the family room, or Plan B with sight lines to the family room window and another through the living room to a well-placed dining room window? These sight lines make Plan B feel larger.

Try to make your way to the kitchen through the family room of Plan A. You'll have to negotiate the furniture and probably pass between the sofa and the TV. In Plan B you follow a horizontal band directly to the kitchen. Plan A gives you only two sight lines from the family room: one through the rear windows and one through the breakfast area window. Plan B gives you four: one through the rear windows, one to the breakfast area windows, one into the kitchen, and another to the foyer.

Aside from the passage to the formal dining room, the main access to the kitchen in Plan A is through a 36-inch opening at the breakfast area — an opening that will be partially blocked by the breakfast table and chairs. All traffic in the home is through this congested area. Compare that to Plan B's kitchen access. There are four ways in, out and around the kitchen. Notice the sight lines from the kitchen in Plan A are limited to only two and you're totally cut off from the family room. The utility room and powder room block potential sight lines to the rear yard from the breakfast area and kitchen. Plan B, on the other hand, provides five sight lines from the kitchen and breakfast area. The utility room is tucked conveniently between the kitchen and dining room where it doesn't interfere with potential sight lines.

Compare traffic patterns between the other bedrooms and kitchen in both plans. In Plan A, the placement of the bedrooms requires a diagonal path, navigating through furniture in the family room to get to the kitchen. Plan B makes use of horizontal banding that doesn't interfere with the family room. Every room in Plan B also has better furniture walls than Plan A.

In Plan A only the family room is oriented to the back yard, while in Plan B there are four. Notice how Plan B provides a private wing for the master bedroom, with virtually no common walls. The mid-wall entrance to the master bedroom in Plan A opens this room visually to the family room, besides cutting the space in half, making it "live" smaller.

Plan B also offers more flexibility with the fourth bedroom, which can become a nursery, guest room, hobby area, or sitting area.

Something else that is often overlooked is that secondary bedroom closets in Plan B give you six more feet of usable rod and shelf space. (Walk-in closets are not always better if they don't give you more rod and shelf space.)

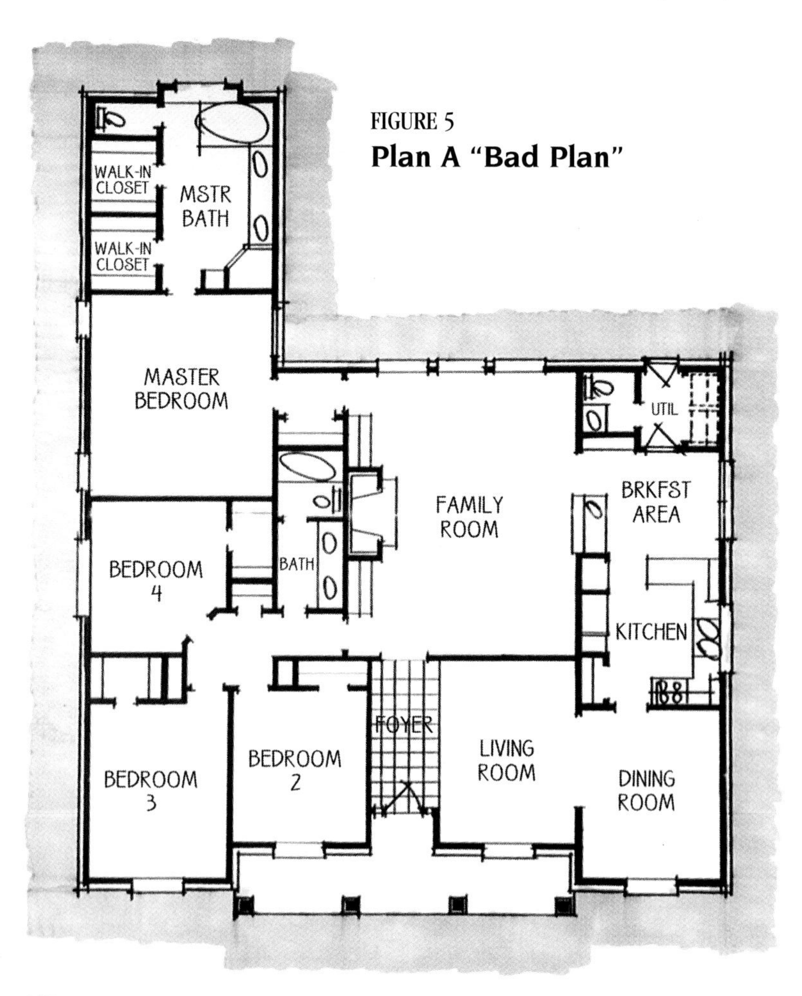

FIGURE 5
Plan A "Bad Plan"

So, as you can see, the differences between two floor plans might seem subtle on paper, but don't be fooled. These differences can have a huge impact on the way you live.

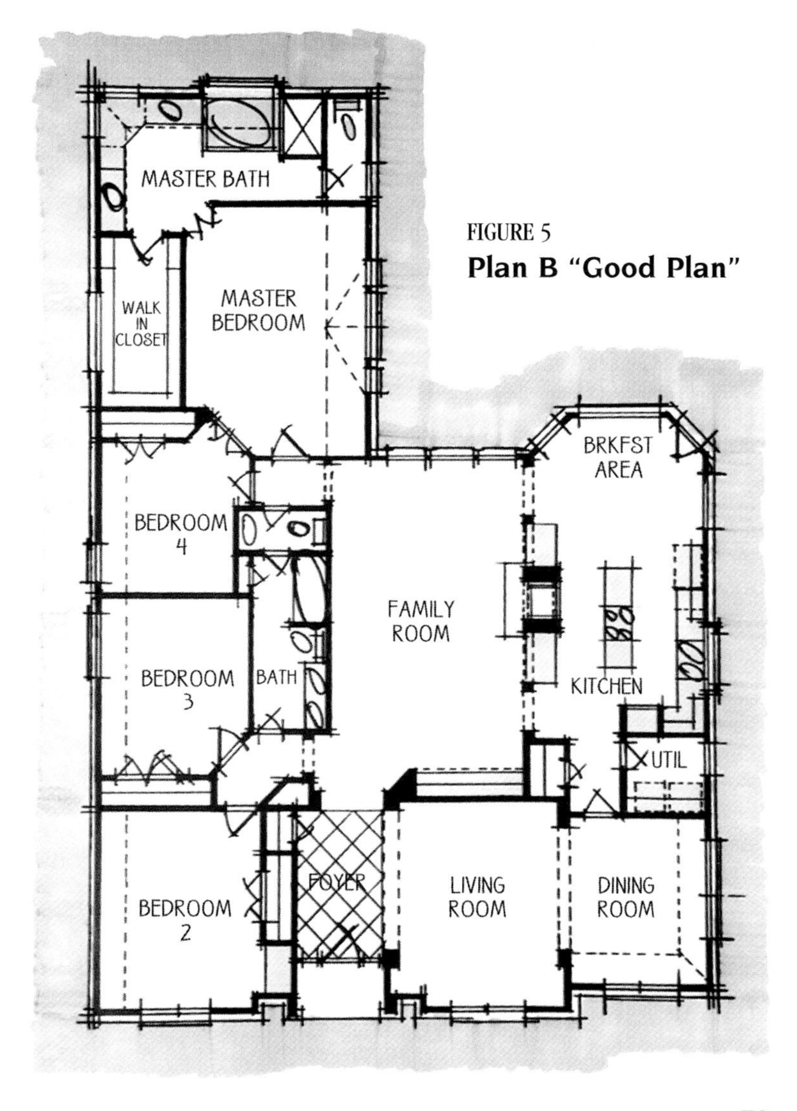

FIGURE 5
Plan B "Good Plan"

CHAPTER SEVEN

The Art of the Deal

OK, LET'S GET THIS OUT OF THE WAY UP FRONT: HALF OF us want the most home for our money; the other half want the most money for our home. Where both halves meet is called "the deal." The best ones look good from both sides of the table.

Fortunately, this isn't the car business where it's us, the lambs, versus them, the wolves: those dreaded car salesmen. The idea of the average consumer walking into a car dealership and doing battle is like watching a third-world country field a basketball team against NBA all-stars: Not a pretty picture.

Home buying is different. Your chances of making a fair deal are far better than when buying a car. If it's a used home, most of us let our hired guns shoot it out. We call them Realtors®. Assuming each side's agent is in the same league, an equitable deal is usually hatched without our ever having to get our hands dirty.

Most people use a Realtor® when buying or selling a used home.

If it's a new home sale, a Realtor® may not be as necessary

because the builder generally sets the price based on his costs for land and construction. If you're relocating — the latest Census says 4,500 households move between states every day — a Realtor's® expertise in evaluating builders and neighborhoods can be very helpful.

Ultimately, it will be up to you to decide what the home is worth and what you're willing to pay. The criteria you use will vary depending on whether you're shopping for a new home or a resale. I've included checklists for both situations.

Factors that determine the value of a resale home

- **The school district**
- **The exterior design and floor plan**
- **The location (access to employment, hospitals, and shopping)**
- **Number of bedrooms and baths**
- **The size of the home**
- **Recent updates (new kitchen or bath)**
- **Window treatments**
- **Lot size**
- **Condition**
- **Landscaping**

Look at what similar homes in the neighborhood are selling for and shoot for something in that range. A home's value can be affected by the condition of homes next door and across the street, too. For example, a remodeled beauty can have its value diminished if it's book-ended by a couple of beasts. Likewise, an ugly duckling will fetch more if it's surrounded by swans.

General housing market conditions will also have a big impact on the price you pay. If it's a buyer's market, meaning there are more homes than buyers, demand will be low and so will prices. A seller's market is when there are more buyers than homes, driving up prices. Rising mortgage interest rates can create a buyer's market, while falling rates tend to produce a seller's market. As unlikely as it may sound, your best time to buy might be in a rising interest

Your best time to buy might be when interest rates are rising.

rate market when there may be more sellers than buyers, so you can make a better "deal." Just get an adjustable rate mortgage and refinance when interest rates come back down.

One other important ingredient in the success of your deal is our old friend, time. Whoever has more of it usually has the upper hand. If the seller gets the notion that you have to move quickly, he or she will be less likely to negotiate, so try not to show any urgency until the price is set.

If you have a home to sell, you may consider a contingency contract for the home you are purchasing. This basically says you will buy this home if and when your current home can be sold. If the seller accepts a contingency contract, then you've given yourself a little peace of mind because you don't have to worry about making two mortgage payments should your current home not sell. Many sellers won't accept a contingency sale for the same reason because they can't control the outcome. Your best chance of getting a contingency sale is during a buyer's market, where more sellers are competing for fewer buyers.

Factors that determine the value of a new home

- **The school district**
- **The builder's reputation and stability**
- **The exterior design and floor plan**
- **Number of bedrooms and baths**
- **The total square footage of air conditioned space**
- **Porches and other amenities**
- **Special features**
- **A well-defined process for making selections, choosing options and upgrades**
- **The location (access to employment, hospitals, and shopping)**
- **A good warranty program**

If you're shopping for a new home, time can work to your advantage. Be sure to look at recently completed homes first. The builder could be paying as much as 1% of the sales price per month in carrying costs for interest, taxes, and maintenance, making him more flexible on the price. Don't get carried away, though. Builders don't make as much on their homes as you might think — usually 5% before taxes. It's unlikely they will be willing to forfeit a good lot and spend six months building a home only to break even.

Don't overlook the builder's reputation when comparing homes, either. The more reputable the builder, the more marketable — and valuable — the home will be.

Personally Speaking...

IF THIS IS YOUR FIRST HOME BUYING EXPERIENCE, you've probably noticed it's getting increasingly difficult to sleep as the big day draws near. Try to relax. Yes, it's a big step. But it's a step most successful Americans make in their lives. And you'll survive.

I'll never forget how nervous Bonnie and I were when we bought our first house. Like most people these days, it took both of our incomes to qualify for the loan and the monthly payments made my palms sweat. Sixty days after we moved in I was fired from my job (yes, it happens to the best of us). Fortunately we were able to sell within a couple of months and we made out all right. Just do your homework (are you tired of hearing me say that yet?) and you can survive those detours and bumps in the road. I'm living proof!

Check the classifieds for resales. If you find the builder's name is used as a selling point, then chances are pretty good that he is a respected builder.

It's a lot to think about, but don't be discouraged. Very few of us are Donald Trumps, yet we manage to survive. Just take your time, bookmark this chapter, and you'll have no problem mastering the art of the deal.

Notes

CHAPTER EIGHT

Show Me the Money

EVERY INDUSTRY HAS ITS LANGUAGE. I DON'T GOLF, BUT MY friends who do tell me they slice it, pull it, push it, hook it, shank it, let the big dog eat and, sometimes end up at granny's house with a snowman. Not knowing the vernacular can be intimidating. Before we go any further, let's take some of the mystery out of mortgagespeak.

Like everything in life, money has its price. With mortgages, it's expressed in interest rates, discount points, and origination fees. You must understand each of these terms because they comprise the true price of your mortgage.

We all know that interest is the fee for borrowing money. It's not the only fee, but it's by far the largest cost of your purchase. (Over a 30-year mortgage, the total interest is far more than the purchase price of your home.) Don't try to multiply the loan amount by the interest rate to determine your total payments. That would be too easy. Mortgage interest is calculated daily on the original principal balance plus the accrued and unpaid interest. Remember that business math course you took to avoid calculus? If not,

Interest expense is by far the single largest cost of buying a home.

don't worry about it. That's why we have the Internet and payment calculators. Check out the Fannie Mae web site at www.homepath.com.

When dealing with mortgage interest, little things can mean a lot. For example, let's assume you borrow $120,000 at 7.5%. Your monthly principal and interest payments would be $839.06 for a 30-year mortgage. Over the life of the loan, you will have paid $182,061 in interest. For an additional $274 per month you can pay off the same $120,000 in 15 years and save $102,000 in interest. During the first year of a 30-year mortgage you will have paid $1,106 toward the principal versus $4,501 with a 15-year loan.

Needless to say, most of us are better off with a 15-year mortgage because it costs less and builds equity faster. If the payments on a 15-year loan are too steep at first, you can always start with a 30-year mortgage and make extra principal payments as you can afford them. Those payments will then go 100% toward paying down the principal, significantly reducing the cost of your loan.

Another way to lower your monthly payments is to buy down the interest rate with discount points. Discount points are equal to 1% of the loan amount and are what the mortgage company charges for a lower interest rate.

Typically, one discount point will reduce the interest rate by at least .25%. So, if the current interest rate is 7.5%, you could pay one point to get a 7.25% mortgage. This cuts your principal and interest payment from $839.06 to $818.61. That's a savings of $20.45 per month. It would take almost five years (58.6 months) for the savings to cover the $1,200. If you're planning to live there more than five years and you have the $1,200, it could be worth it. (Assuming the interest rates are so low that you know you wouldn't want to refinance.)

Another option may be an adjustable rate mortgage or ARM. With an ARM, your monthly payments start out low the first year and fluctuate thereafter. The first thing to look for with an ARM is a good rate cap — the limit it can be increased within a given period of time. The cap should always be on the interest rate — not the monthly payment — and it should be tied to an independent, third party rate that the lender does not control, usually one-year U.S. Treasury bills, which are published daily in *The Wall Street Journal*. It should also specify the maximum interest rate you will pay for the life of the loan.

Remember that the introductory rate is only good for the first year and that it — and your monthly payment —

will go up (unless interest rates take a nosedive). To get a feel for next year's payments, ask the lender what they would be if they adjusted the rate today.

As a rule of thumb, you would choose an ARM when interest rates are high or if your career requires you to move frequently. Do not use it to purchase a house you could not otherwise afford.

So, how much home can you afford? Historically, mortgage companies have used fairly standard criteria when determining what size mortgage you qualify for: They will usually allow house payments up to 28% of your monthly household gross income for the house payment alone and approximately 36% for all of your payments, including the house, the car, student loans, and credit cards, etc. These days, though, Fannie Mae and Freddie Mac guidelines allow for more flexibility, so many lenders have dropped the ratio method in favor of credit scoring systems.

Mortgage companies today use credit scoring to determine the loan amount consumers qualify for.

There are three national credit bureaus (Experion,

Trans Union, and Equifax) that use a credit scoring system. The consumer is given a rating, which is made up of payment history, open credit card accounts, and the number of credit cards that are "maxed out." A rating of 680 or greater is considered A+ credit. The lender will be far more lenient with consumers who have this rating.

In the final analysis, you are the best judge of what you can afford. Although I don't recommend becoming house poor, keep in mind that your income is likely to go up in relationship to your house payment, so writing that check to the mortgage company every month will become more comfortable as time goes by.

Other Closing Costs

The mortgage company's charge for providing the loan is called the origination fee. Currently, the industry standard is equal to 1% of the loan amount. You will also be required to purchase title insurance. Title insurance protects the lender and you from any loss that could occur due to disputes over the

Because closing costs can vary widely, it's always a good idea to get firm quotes up front.

ownership of your property. The other charges that will be paid at closing can vary widely and include the application fee, credit report, appraisal, survey, inspections, attorneys' fees, court house recording fees, messenger fees — even charges for photocopies. These are the fees that will help you narrow your selection of lenders from those offering similar interest rates. Be sure to get firm quotes in writing on these fees because they can add up to a lot of money.

Choosing a Lender

Let's begin with an overview of what deals are out there. At this stage you want to survey the market and come up with a short list of eligible lenders. Start by asking friends whom they recommend and, more importantly, whom they would not recommend. Then, if you have a lot of time, let your fingers do the walking through the Yellow Pages. If not, surf the Internet and check the business section of your Sunday newspaper. Be sure to compare apples with apples. You should, if possible, contact those lenders and request a quote for a 60-day closing (less if you are planning to move sooner). Since lenders typically do not lock in rates for longer than 60 days, you must get a 60-day rate quote to compare real rates.

Pay close attention to the estimated closing costs and whether they are listed on the buyer's side or the seller's side — this varies from state to state. You're looking for the lowest interest rates offered at comparable discount points, origination fees, and miscellaneous charges.

If you will be shopping for a new home, don't overlook a mortgage company that regularly works with the home-builder. Often you can benefit from the relationship because the lender has a vested interest in satisfying the builder and his clients. Communication between the mortgage company and your builder may also be better, making the whole process more efficient.

Mortgage companies typically adjust their rates daily based on the yield on Federal National Mortgage Association (Fannie Mae), Federal Home Loan Mortgage Corp. (Freddie Mac) and Government National Mortgage Association (Ginnie Mae) mortgage-backed securities published in *The Wall Street Journal*. Keep in mind that what you see today could change by Tuesday. All you're looking for here is a ranking of the top five deals.

The next step is to contact each lender for their current rates. Ask them for a good faith estimate, in writing, of their closing costs. Let them know you are shopping and ask them how long they can lock in the rate quoted — that is, the number of days you have to close the deal before the rate changes. Usually, depending on the rate, the lender will lock it in for anywhere from 30 to 60 days. If they won't lock in a rate for as long as you need it, find out what their current mortgage quotes are based on — one-year treasury bills on ARMs, for example. If they are quoting rates that are 2.75% over the one-year average treasury bills today, ask if they will commit to staying within 2.75% of them, regardless of your closing date. Again, check their 60-day quotes. This is important because some lenders have been known to "bait and switch" by getting you in the door with a low current rate that cannot be locked in and then raising it substantially at closing.

Finally, check out the company's track record by asking for references, and don't overlook your own gut feelings. When it's all said and done, you will have shared a lot of personal financial information with these people. Choosing the "cheapest" mortgage company may not be as important as finding one you can trust.

CHAPTER NINE

Dream Homes Are Built By Dream Builders

How to choose the best builder

THERE IS NO BAR EXAM TO BECOME A HOMEBUILDER. You don't even need to own a hammer, much less know how to use one. When it comes to the greatest investment of our lives it's caveat emptor — let the buyer beware. Before you begin your home search, before you allow yourself to fall in love with a home, find out everything you can about the company that's building it. When you buy a new home, you're really buying that builder's experience, integrity, and reputation.

Start with a list of builders who build the style of home you like where you want to live. If it's in a new community, often the developer limits your choice to a select few. If your target area is broader or if you plan to build on your own lot, drive that area of town and look for builders' signs. Check the weekend newspaper for ads and listings. Search the Internet for your city's homebuilder association web site and look for members who build in your area of interest.

Make a list of those builders who build where you want to live.

Show this list to everyone — friends, coworkers, neighbors, your barber, the postman — and ask them what they know about these builders. You want the good, the bad and the ugly. Any builder who elicits more than a couple of negative responses from your panel of experts should be crossed off the list.

Next, start driving. Visit the neighborhoods where these builders' homes are and interview a minimum of three homeowners from each builder you are considering. Ask them about the builder's strengths and weaknesses. What did they like best? What did they like least? Would they recommend him to others? Talk to Realtors® in the area and get their opinions. Any builder who gets a couple of bad reviews should get the ax.

Check your newspaper's real estate classified section for resales to see if the builder's name is mentioned as a selling point in the ads. Drive by the builders' older homes and see how they are maintaining. Is

Talk to Realtors® in the area and get their opinions.

the architectural style still appealing or is it dated?

By now, your list of candidates should be narrowed down to a manageable few. Visit their sales offices and tour their model homes, if they have any. Talk to the sales consultant and ask why this builder is special. Have they received any industry recognition and awards? Look for a good variety of floor plans and options. Do the people seem to enjoy what they do? At this stage, if everyone you meet isn't friendly and helpful, the chances are good that things will only go downhill from here, so walk away and look for a builder who wants your business and acts like it.

Ask about their warranty program to find out how they take care of their homeowners after the sale. Have they devoted a whole team to warranty, repairs, and follow-up, or does it sound like a subject that doesn't interest them?

Ask builders about their warranty programs.

Drive by their homes under construction to see how

they build. If you don't know what to look for, try taking along someone who does. In general, you're looking for solid materials, good craftsmanship, square angles, and straight lines and a clean job site.

There are plenty of professional homebuilders who know their craft and who stand behind their homes. Unfortunately, there are also some bad apples out there. You don't have to let one spoil your dreams of the perfect home. Just remember to consider the builder before you consider his homes.

Beware of the "price-per-square-foot" trap

Price-per-square-foot is determined by dividing the price of the house by the total square feet. A 2,500 square-foot home selling for $250,000 costs $100 per square foot. Assuming you now understand how to do the math, please file this skill in that compartment of your brain labeled "Useless Information." Price-per-square-foot can be helpful as an average when comparing one community to another, but anyone who compares one home to another on this basis is making a huge mis-

Hardwood flooring costs more per square foot than carpeting or vinyl.

take. After all, you don't buy cars based on price-per-pound.

There are far too many variables in homebuilding to take such a broad-brushed approach. What kind of materials and craftsmanship were used?

Hardwood flooring costs more than carpeting and vinyl. Solid wood cabinets cost more than particleboard. Are the ceilings ten feet high or eight feet? Two-story homes are often cheaper to build than one-stories with the same square footage.

Location plays a large role, too. Is the lot over-sized with trees? Is the neighborhood convenient to good schools, employment, shopping and hospitals?

How good is the floor plan? Does it have good sight lines, traffic patterns, and room placement? (See *Reading Between the Lines* in Chapter 6.)

Think about it. If price-per-square-foot was how we judged our home purchases, we'd all be living in tents.

Satisfy your urge to comparison shop by unit price at the grocery store or gas station. It's not a smart way to buy a home.

What about hiring an architect?

The vast majority of architects make their living in commercial design — schools, churches, shopping malls, and office buildings. Less than 10% of new homes are designed by a homebuyer-hired architect.

Architects and Home Designers (they both do the same thing, the difference is that an "Architect" has been licensed by the state) have experience and knowledge in designing homes for customers. Those customers who usually go to an architect are building homes that are $750,000 and up and they want one-of-a-kind homes. I would not go to an architect for a more reasonably priced home because:

■ Builders have lots of experience designing, building, and selling homes. Their homes must consistently meet a broad range of customers' needs or they won't succeed. If I buy a builder's home, I don't have to worry as much about owning a home that won't sell due to individual whims and desires.

■ Builders have thousands of consumers who give input to improve their designs. We are constantly tweaking plans to be the best they can be.

■ Builders also have a community of industry experts to help improve plans — from Realtors®, competitors, sales associates, developers, etc. All these people pulling together make builders' designs better and better.

■ Builders can give me more for my money. They are experts at building cost-efficient designs that give me a lot of visual "bang for my buck."

■ I get a list of specifications (i.e.: insulation thickness, trim type, cabinet type, etc.). This information is sometimes not available on an architect's set of plans.

■ I can often see real-life examples of the plan I choose. I can compare specifications and designs to choose the best builder for me.

■ Paying an architect's fee all by myself is more expensive than having the cost of plans spread among many homebuyers. Also, builders will usually get better prices from an architect than an individual customer will.

■ Some architects are not as practical as builders

(often in response to their customers' requests) and might design a dream home that will give the average customer nightmares.

■ Often, an architect's plans don't include all the specifics that a builder needs to make a proper bid, which means I'm unable to make an apples-to-apples comparison of builders.

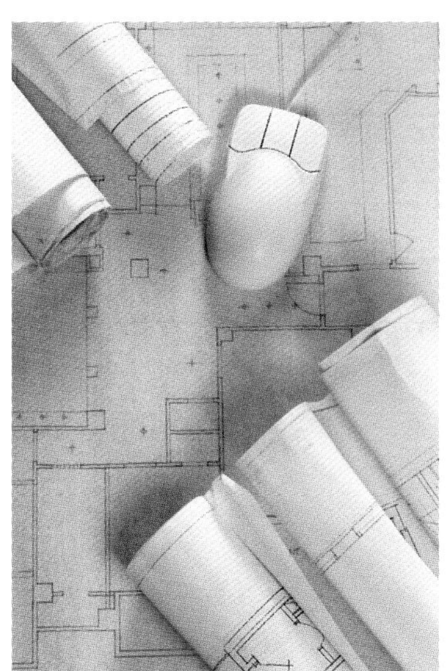

Architects' plans often don't include all the specifications a builder needs.

■ When problems arise during construction, I might get stuck in the middle of a finger-pointing contest between the architect and the builder, in which no one accepts responsibility.

There are plenty of times when it does make sense to use an architect — very specific design taste, special needs, one-of-a-kind lot, you have a big budget — but for my money, I'll take the convenience, efficiency, expertise, and sizzle that a builder offers any day.

CHAPTER TEN

Hidden Treasures and Hidden Costs

What you see is not always what you get

FOR MANY LARGE HOMEBUILDERS, THE BEST SALES TOOL they have is the model home. Properly done, a model home can showcase a builder's design and construction quality while helping the buyer visualize living in the home. It's often cited as a major factor in the consumer's final decision. It should come as no surprise that many builders invest heavily in their model homes. (Some spend as much as $100,000 on furnishings and decorations alone.) Though it's not always intentional, it inevitably leads to confusion and frustration for the homebuyer. The builders want their homes to "show" as well as possible. If you want a better feel for what you're buying, walk through some of the builder's recently completed, unsold homes.

Before you tour the model home, always ask the sales consultant for a list of what's not included and how much extra it costs. That way you can avoid setting your expectations too high (or even worse, choosing one builder over another because you think you're getting more for your money).

Also, who will be your primary contact for the entire process of buying and/or building your home? Will it be the overly-friendly salesperson? Or, once you've signed the contract, will you be introduced to the grumpy construction superintendent who thinks his job would be terrific if it weren't for you pesky customers? The best solution is when the builder assigns a team of professionals who are focused on your needs. The top builders in any given market can attract and retain talented individuals who have a true passion for their work and understand the importance of customer satisfaction.

Always ask the sales person what's not included and how much extra it costs.

Ask to meet everyone on the team responsible for your home, and make sure you can get along with them. That includes other sales people who might fill in during vacations, administrative assistants, contractors, the builder, warranty personnel, decorators, the supervisor — anyone who could potentially ruin your day. If you don't feel comfortable, ask for a replacement. Also, be sure to get the name and phone number of the manager of the area in case you run into problems later. This may be just another house to them, but for you it's one of life's great moments that should be relished. Don't let anyone rain on your parade.

Ask to meet everyone who will be responsible for your home's completion.

While you're adding up the extras, the easiest things to overlook are window coverings and landscaping. Some builders include a modest budget for a front yard, but you might want more trees and shrubs than the plan specifies. You might also want a backyard privacy fence, if one isn't included.

I've seen people struggle with their wallpaper and flooring selections for weeks, sometimes delaying the completion of their home, then move in and tack up blankets and sheets over the windows. Nothing detracts from an otherwise lovely home like not having window coverings.

Naturally, brick and paint selections, carpeting, and

other permanent fixtures are important and should take priority over things you can do after you move in, but all too often — in their focus on other more pressing issues — homeowners wake up the morning after to an urgent need for privacy. Think ahead. Budget at least something for those windows where privacy is needed immediately, like bathrooms and bedrooms. Then you can add more to the rest of the home as you can afford it.

Other potential hidden costs can come from construction delays and interest rate lock-ins. With a process as complex as homebuilding, there is no shortage of things that can delay construction (See Chapter 11), creating a domino effect that can lead to unexpected costs. If you're selling a home and have to move, you may need to rent a place to live and store your things in the interim. You may have locked in that too-good-to-be-true interest rate with the 60-day lock only to discover that you won't make the deadline and

You may need a place to store your things if there are unexpected construction delays.

rates have gone up a point. Don't lock in your rate or confirm your move until about 30 days from when the builder estimates you can close and move in.

As they say, that's life. There's very little you can do about unexpected twists of fate, other than try to have a contingency plan, a sense of humor, and remind yourself, "it ain't over till it's over," as Yogi Berra says. Besides, you will still have those new home warranties and that nice fat mortgage interest deduction on April 15th.

Notes

CHAPTER ELEVEN

Great Expectations

What to look for during construction

IMAGINE ORDERING A NEW AUTOMOBILE AND THEN VISITING the assembly plant every day to check on its progress. As silly as that may sound, it is precisely what we expect when having a home built. What other purchase do you make that entitles you to supervise the manufacturing process so closely?

Building a home is a complex proposition. It's not performed in a climate-controlled factory with construction materials inventoried on-site. Homebuilding happens outdoors, usually over a period of five to ten months, with crews and materials arriving on-site as needed. Although there are some similarities, each home is a unique product, specifically designed with an immense investment of thought and energy. There are literally thousands of things that must happen in a given order with meticulous inspections along the way, which means there are thousands of things that can go

The greatest challenge in home building is setting and meeting customers' expectations.

wrong (not to mention acts of God over which neither you nor the builder has any control). No wonder the greatest challenge in homebuilding is setting and meeting customer expectations.

You signed the contract on your new home three months ago and everything has gone so smoothly that you told the people who are buying your old house that they can take possession in 45 days. That also happens to be how long you've locked in the interest rate for on your new mortgage. Now you're relaxing in your favorite chair, watching the local weather on the 6 o'clock news, when you learn that El Niño or La Niña or La Vida Loca has thrown off major global weather patterns and that your neck of the woods is in for a little shower that shouldn't last more than 40 days and 40 nights and...this just in: a tornado strikes a factory in a town you've never heard of, until your builder tells you that's where the windows were being made for your new home...turning to business news...the Federal Reserve Chairman, in an effort to curb inflation, has announced another interest rate hike, this one the largest in history, which will cause mortgage interest rates to increase dramatically.

Hey, it could happen. Stay flexible and keep your move-in date adjustable. This is not the time to paint yourself into a corner.

Home Placement

Do you know which direction your lot faces? Where does the sun rise in winter? Where will it set in the summer? What about the prevailing breezes? Do you know that in any given area — due to geographic features and climatic conditions — winds will generally come from the same direction? Do you have a copy of city, county, and neighborhood restrictions? What are the minimum and maximum "set-backs" — the distance your home may be from the street and property lines?

Choose your views. A slight variation in the placement of your home can make a world of difference. It's not just what you see, sometimes it's what you don't see. Siting with respect to trees and other vertical obstructions can help you avoid eyesores like utility lines, water towers, or other houses.

Properly siting your home can help you avoid eyesores and obstructions.

Depending on the size and location of your lot, your choices might be limited, but don't treat this stage lightly. Ask questions. Investigate. Home siting can have a significant impact on your home's curb appeal and resale value.

The construction process

The first thing to look for during construction is a well-defined process. You should be given an outline of what to expect at each of the various stages of construction, as well as a schedule of meetings with the builder or superintendent.

This would be a good time to start a construction binder. Using a three-ring binder with tabbed dividers and pockets, start collecting all construction information about your new home: literature and details from meetings with plumbing and lighting fixture suppliers, paint color swatches, wallpaper and carpeting samples, and notes from meetings with your builder. Be sure to have your builder give you quotes on any changes you make that will affect the construction cost (you might be surprised how quickly these little "hickeys" can add up).

You should expect to meet with the builder prior to breaking ground to go over all options, selections and any last-minute changes to the plans. You should meet prior to the drywall stage to review framing, electrical, and plumbing items. There should also be a meeting scheduled prior to closing to compare notes and discuss any last minute changes.

Naturally, you will visit the construction site often to monitor progress. If you see something that looks out of place or wrong, contact the builder immediately. Don't assume he has seen it, too. Probably no one has studied the plans of your new home as closely as you have, and no one else will have to live with the mistakes. Catching them early will waste less time and money than waiting until other stages have begun and having to call back subcontractors who have already left the job.

Do pay close attention to the finishing detail. You don't have to be an experienced builder to see that crown molding joints have gaps; that sheet rock isn't aligned properly; that paint is sloppy; or that carpeting is not spliced neatly. Compare the finishes in your home to those in the builder's model home. You have every right to expect the same level of quality.

Don't be overly concerned if you see little or no activity some days. It is normal for there to be gaps between one crew finishing and the next one's arrival. There are also inspections that must be made by the city, and inspectors are not always available when needed. Besides these construction-related delays, you can also encounter a spell of bad weather. Don't schedule things too tightly. Give yourself as large a window as possible for moving in and for interest rate lock-ins — a minimum of 30 days, preferably 60 days' leeway.

It's normal for there to be gaps in construction activity.

The construction process will find you on a roller coaster of emotions. Some days you'll be on top of the world; other days you'll wonder how things could get any worse. Just try to remember that this gamut of emotions from elation to frustration is a normal part of homebuilding; we all go through it to some degree. Your experience will depend largely on how well your expectations are met. I've learned that there are two types of home-

Everyone experiences highs and lows during the construction process.

builders: those whose businesses are based on satisfying customers and those who just want to take the money and run. I suggest you choose the former. There are also two kinds of homebuyers: those who set their expectations unreasonably high and those who don't. They both end up with the same quality of home; it's just that those with realistic expectations enjoy the process a lot more.

Notes

CHAPTER TWELVE

Interior Design

How to make it look as good as the model

IF YOUR BUILDER HAS FULLY-FURNISHED MODEL HOMES THEN you've seen what your home could look like if you ever win the Lotto. Based on the current odds of winning the big one — somewhere around 11 billion to one — maybe you should look at more economical ways to feather your nest.

The first step is to determine how long you will live there. If you know that — because of imminent job transfers, a fast upward career path, a growing family, or an inability just to stay put — you will not be living here longer than say, three to five years, you are a short-timer. If, on the other hand, you plan to grow old and retire in this home, you're in the category of long-timers (most of us fall somewhere between these two extremes). As you might suspect, short-timers and long-timers should make different design choices.

For example, if you're a long-timer, look at major, construction-stage items like optional rooms and additions, pre-wiring for audio and electrical alarms, hardwood or tile flooring, built-in entertainment cabinets, kitchen cabinet expansions, various window and door placement changes, and fireplace modifications. Things of this nature are very expensive and inconvenient to add after closing.

Always keep in mind that you still have landscaping, exterior upgrades, and window coverings to purchase. Try to avoid rolling these costs into your mortgage, if possible. Although it doesn't seem to add that much to the monthly payment, you'll end up paying three to four times the actual cost over the course of the mortgage. If you can't afford to pay cash, many suppliers offer better payment plans than paying interest for 30 years.

If you're a short-timer, go ahead and roll the window coverings and landscaping into the mortgage. They'll probably make the house easier to resell and you won't be there long enough to have paid the full finance costs. Short-timers should design a home they will enjoy living in, one that says something about their taste and lifestyle. Inexpensive and effective design elements that give your home personality and instant appeal include: strong paint colors, wallpaper, chair rails, molding, and

Try to budget a reasonable amount for landscaping and window coverings.

stylish lighting. These are all items that can be easily changed by you or the future owner when it's time to sell.

One of the least expensive and most effective ways to personalize your home is with accent painting — that is, choosing a complimentary color for a wall or trim that "accents" the room. The only rooms a buyer should pay the builder to accent paint are those that will be carpeted; the paint can be applied prior to carpet installation to avoid possible staining and damage. In rooms with hardwoods and tile, independent painters frequently can be less expensive. This can also be an easy do-it-yourself project that's fun for the family.

Accent painting is a cost-effective way to personalize your home.

Here are some other general tips for long and short-timers that seem obvious but can be overlooked in all the excitement of building your home:

- Get a floor plan and make sure your furniture, new or existing, will fit the rooms.

■ Consider furniture placement when locating cable jacks and outlets.

■ Create an "Idea File" with photos of ideas you like clipped from magazines and catalogs.

■ Create a "Colors & Textures Portfolio" that tracks all design choices from paint color and wallpaper to flooring and cabinets.

■ When selecting window shapes, remember arches and irregular shapes cost more to cover than standard rectangular windows, but inevitably add excitement to the home.

■ Measure, re-measure, and measure again.

If you're color-blind or aesthetically-challenged, consider paying for two or three hours of consultation with a professional interior designer. Your new home might never match those expensively-furnished builder models, but you'd be surprised how close you can come even without winning the Lotto.

CHAPTER THIRTEEN

Closing and Moving In

YOU'RE DOWN TO THE FINAL STRETCH. THERE ARE SEVERAL loose ends, but if everyone would just show up and do their jobs, you could move in within a week. Maybe if you go ahead and schedule the closing the builder will pick up the pace and finish things. If not, hey, he can just wrap it all up after you've moved in. No problemo. After all, they're just little things and you're really anxious to move in. "What would be wrong with that?" you ask. In a word, everything.

I know the final days of construction often feel like you're herding baby ducks, but don't give in now. You don't want your builder and his crew taking shortcuts that you'll have to live with for years because you didn't want to wait a few more days. So, repeat after me, "I will not move in until everything is completed." This should become your mantra during the final weeks of construction. When you feel your blood pressure elevating and that little surge of adrenaline makes

Resist the temptation to move into your home before it is completed.

you want to grab a hammer and finish something (or someone) back up, take several deep breaths and say it again, "I will not move in until everything is completed."

If you do move into an unfinished house, be prepared to stay at home waiting for carpenters, plumbers, and other tradesmen who, when they do show up, will not always show up on time. When they finally do arrive, they will disrupt your life, dirty your house, and maybe damage your furniture. Trust me: You don't want that. Let them get out before you move in.

Once everything has been completed to your satisfaction, it's closing time. That means you will sign your name more times than a movie star on Hollywood Boulevard. You've never seen so many forms before and, after a severe case of writer's cramp, you will never want to see them again.

The good news is that you will be sent all the paperwork at least 24 hours prior to closing. This will allow you to check all the figures, con-

You will be given all the closing papers to review in advance.

sult your attorney and/or Realtor®, and — if you're suffering from insomnia — reading all this can help you get a good night's sleep.

The most useful of the forms is the Closing Statement. This itemizes all of the charges and fees, and shows the interest rate as well as the Annual Percentage Rate or APR. This is the effective rate when you factor in other points and fees associated with the loan. You'll want to go over the Closing Statement carefully and make sure it reiterates your understanding of the deal. If necessary, contact the closing officer at the title company where you will close and request clarification and/or corrections.

A Deed of Trust and Title Policy will be part of the paperwork you receive at closing.

You will also be given a copy of the loan agreement, the Deed of Trust, and the Title Policy. These you will also want to examine carefully. There is also a form — I am not making this up — that says your signature is your signature (you've got to sign that one, too).

Don't allow the sea of paperwork to intimidate you. It's fairly routine and regulated. At this point, you will have already agreed to the home's price and mortgage terms. This is just your opportunity to be asked, "Is that your final answer?" and to practice signing your name. If you need more than 24 hours to review the papers, just let the title company know so they can schedule your closing accordingly.

After closing, remember to notify any companies who regularly send you mail and magazines of your new address. Don't forget to turn in a change-of-address form with the post office. Be sure to have the utilities transferred to your name and make sure they are working before moving.

This is also a good time to read all of your warranty papers and appliance instructions. You'll want to keep them together and accessible for the first few months after you move in.

Even though you thoroughly checked everything in, on, and around the home before closing, there are just some things you can't possibly see until you start living there.

You might want to keep a pad and pencil handy the first few days and start a list for your builder. Then one call can cover several items, rather than having him come every day as you notice small things. Obviously, if there is a problem that is dangerous or can lead to greater property damage, you should call him at once.

Finally, there are three things in life that are certain: death, taxes, and buyer's remorse: that feeling in the pit of your stomach that says you just made a big mistake. Don't take it too seriously. Buyer's remorse is normal and not fatal. The symptoms usually fade shortly after you remember how much research and planning went into this decision; that, even if you did make a mistake, the history of appreciation in housing makes this a pretty safe investment.

Notes

CHAPTER FOURTEEN

I Can't Get No Satisfaction

Getting your builder's attention after the sale

FIRST OF ALL, IF YOU FOLLOW MY ADVICE IN CHAPTERS 2, 4, and 9 you can skip this chapter. You probably won't have any trouble getting your builder to respond because you've selected a reputable builder who knows his continued success is directly tied to his customers' satisfaction.

With that said, even the best builders can occasionally make mistakes. The larger ones often have several superintendents and subcontractors, each of whom might be building as many as eight or ten homes at any given time. Your best scenario is to have chosen a builder who has dedicated an entire department to warranty repairs. Good builders usually do, and not because their homes are any more likely to need repairs. They understand how important it is to handle warranty issues promptly and efficiently so that the homeowner can spend less time worrying and more time talking about their wonderful builder (word-of-mouth is the most valuable form of advertising a builder has).

There are things you can do to ensure the best possible service. If you've chosen a top builder who issues a warranty maintenance manual, read the appropriate section and fill out the service request form. It's always advisable to make your requests in writing to avoid misunderstandings. Obviously, this doesn't apply if you're standing in a foot of water from a major plumbing problem. Then you have my permission to use the phone, but follow up in writing when it's convenient. "In writing" doesn't mean you have to wait several days for snail mail. You can e-mail it or fax it.

If you request warranty repairs, make sure you put it in writing.

While I'm on the subject of writing, here's another little secret that works in every industry, but can be especially effective in homebuilding: Don't wait for a problem to write. Write a letter when things go right. Ask any banker about the best time to borrow money. They'll all tell you "If you wait to borrow money until you need it, you've waited too long." It's the same with homebuilding. Catch your builder doing something right and write a letter telling him so. It's like money in the bank. By acknowledging a job well done you show that you're paying attention and that you appreciate his efforts. Another good form of insurance is to refer business to your builder and let him know about it. Later, when you need help and another homeowner who constantly complains needs help, guess who he'll get to first?

If you don't have a manual, check your warranty file (remember chapter 13?), review the paperwork, and follow the directions. Often you can deal directly with the manufacturer if it's an appliance problem, or with the sub-contractor if it's an issue with plumbing or electrical. If this doesn't give you satisfactory results, work your way up the "food chain." You probably won't have to go very high before you get results. Remember to be friendly, if possible. As long as the builder believes you are a potential "word-of-mouth" candidate, it is in his best interest to keep you happy. If he feels you are hopelessly disgruntled, he could adopt a "lost cause" attitude and make your life miserable.

Your best chance of getting satisfactory service from your builder after closing comes from keeping the relationship as positive as possible. Not only will you be taken care of after closing, you'll also continue to get help well outside the warranty period.

Notes

CHAPTER FIFTEEN

Conclusion

CHANCES ARE, IF YOU'RE READING THIS BOOK, YOU'RE READY to ride the home buying roller coaster of emotions. Buckle up. Your ride will take you through excitement, frustration, inspiration, confusion, humility, exhilaration, challenge, remorse, and comfort.

If this is your first home-buying experience, I hope this book has taken some of the mystery out of it for you. For those of you who've been through it before, maybe you'll be better-prepared this time.

Buying a home is a rite of passage, a monumental threshold that, if you are fortunate enough to cross, will forever change your life and your concept of what home is. No longer will home be that place where you grew up; from closing day on it will become a symbol of your hopes, your dreams, your sense of who you are.

It will be that very special place you've chosen to shelter the ones you care about the most. It will be your weekend project for more weekends than you can imagine. It will test you and it will teach you. It will make you crazy. It will make you proud.

Dorothy was right. There's no place like home.

Glossary of Real Estate Terms

Reprinted by permission of Fannie Mae

Thanks to the folks at Fannie Mae for letting me use their glossary. It will help you understand most of the terms you'll encounter during your home-shopping adventure. However, I must warn you. Glossaries are like dictionaries. They are not meant to be read entirely in one sitting unless you suffer from insomnia. Please do not attempt to read it while driving or operating heavy machinery.

acceleration clause
A provision in a mortgage that gives the lender the right to demand payment of the entire principal balance if a monthly payment is missed.

acceptance
An offeree's consent to enter into a contract and be bound by the terms of the offer.

additional principal payment
A payment by a borrower of more than the scheduled principal amount due in order to reduce the remaining balance on the loan.

adjustable-rate mortgage (ARM)
A mortgage that permits the lender to adjust its interest rate periodically on the basis of changes in a specified index.

adjusted basis

The original cost of a property plus the value of any capital expenditures for improvements to the property minus any depreciation taken.

adjustment date

The date on which the interest rate changes for an adjustable-rate mortgage (ARM).

adjustment period

The period that elapses between the adjustment dates for an adjustable-rate mortgage (ARM).

administrator

A person appointed by a probate court to administer the estate of a person who died intestate.

affordability analysis

A detailed analysis of your ability to afford the purchase of a home. An affordability analysis takes into consideration your income, liabilities, and available funds, along with the type of mortgage you plan to use, the area where you want to purchase a home, and the closing costs that you might expect to pay.

amenity

A feature of real property that enhances its attractiveness and increases the occupant's or user's satisfaction although the feature is not essential to the property's use. Natural amenities include a pleasant or desirable location near water, scenic views of the surrounding area, etc. Human-made amenities include swimming pools, tennis courts, community buildings, and other recreational facilities.

amortization

The gradual repayment of a mortgage loan by installments.

amortization schedule

A timetable for payment of a mortgage loan. An amortization schedule shows the amount of each payment applied to interest and principal and shows the remaining balance after each payment is made.

amortization term

The amount of time required to amortize the mortgage loan. The amortization term is expressed as a number of months. For example, for a 30-year fixed-rate mortgage, the amortization term is 360 months.

amortize

To repay a mortgage with regular payments that cover both principal and interest.

annual mortgagor statement

A report sent to the mortgagor each year. The report shows how much was paid in taxes and interest during the year, as well as the remaining mortgage loan balance at the end of the year.

annual percentage rate (APR)

The cost of a mortgage stated as a yearly rate; includes such

items as interest, mortgage insurance, and loan origination fee (points).

annuity

An amount paid yearly or at other regular intervals, often on a guaranteed dollar basis.

application

A form used to apply for a mortgage loan and to record pertinent information concerning a prospective mortgagor and the proposed security.

appraisal

A written analysis of the estimated value of a property prepared by a qualified appraiser. Contrast with home inspection.

appraised value

An opinion of a property's fair market value, based on an appraiser's knowledge, experience, and analysis of the property.

appraiser

A person qualified by education, training, and experience to estimate the value of real property and personal property.

appreciation

An increase in the value of a property due to changes in market conditions or other causes. The opposite of depreciation.

assessed value

The valuation placed on property by a public tax assessor for purposes of taxation.

assessment
The process of placing a value on property for the strict purpose of taxation. May also refer to a levy against property for a special purpose, such as a sewer assessment.

assessment rolls
The public record of taxable property.

assessor
A public official who establishes the value of a property for taxation purposes.

asset
Anything of monetary value that is owned by a person. Assets include real property, personal property, and enforceable claims against others (including bank accounts, stocks, mutual funds, and so on).

assignment
The transfer of a mortgage from one person to another.

assumable mortgage
A mortgage that can be taken over ("assumed") by the buyer when a home is sold.

assumption
The transfer of the seller's existing mortgage to the buyer. See assumable mortgage.

assumption clause
A provision in an assumable mortgage that allows a buyer to

assume responsibility for the mortgage from the seller. The loan does not need to be paid in full by the original borrower upon sale or transfer of the property.

assumption fee

The fee paid to a lender (usually by the purchaser of real property) resulting from the assumption of an existing mortgage.

attorney-in-fact

One who holds a power of attorney from another to execute documents on behalf of the grantor of the power.

B

balance sheet

A financial statement that shows assets, liabilities, and net worth as of a specific date.

balloon mortgage

A mortgage that has level monthly payments that will amortize it over a stated term but that provides for a lump sum payment to be due at the end of an earlier specified term.

balloon payment

The final lump sum payment that is made at the maturity date of a balloon mortgage.

bankrupt

A person, firm, or corporation that, through a court proceeding, is relieved from the payment of all debts after the surrender of all assets to a court-appointed trustee.

bankruptcy

A proceeding in a federal court in which a debtor who owes more than his or her assets can relieve the debts by transferring his or her assets to a trustee.

before-tax income

Income before taxes are deducted.

beneficiary

The person designated to receive the income from a trust, estate, or a deed of trust.

bequeath

To transfer personal property through a will.

betterment

An improvement that increases property value as distinguished from repairs or replacements that simply maintain value.

bill of sale

A written document that transfers title to personal property.

binder

A preliminary agreement, secured by the payment of an earnest money deposit, under which a buyer offers to purchase real estate.

biweekly payment mortgage

A mortgage that requires payments to reduce the debt every two weeks (instead of the standard monthly payment schedule). The 26 (or possibly 27) biweekly payments are each equal to one-half of the monthly payment that would be required if the loan were a standard 30-year fixed-rate mortgage, and they are usually drafted from the borrower's bank account. The result for the borrower is a substantial savings in interest.

blanket insurance policy

A single policy that covers more than one piece of property (or more than one person).

blanket mortgage

The mortgage that is secured by a cooperative project, as opposed to the share loans on individual units within the project.

bona fide

In good faith, without fraud.

bond

An interest-bearing certificate of debt with a maturity date. An obligation of a government or business corporation. A real estate bond is a written obligation usually secured by a mortgage or a deed of trust.

breach

A violation of any legal obligation.

bridge loan

A form of second trust that is collateralized by the borrower's present home (which is usually for sale) in a manner that allows the proceeds to be used for closing on a new house before the present home is sold. Also known as "swing loan."

broker

A person who, for a commission or a fee, brings parties together and assists in negotiating contracts between them. See mortgage broker.

budget

A detailed plan of income and expenses expected over a certain period of time. A budget can provide guidelines for managing future investments and expenses.

budget category

A category of income or expense data that you can use in a budget. You can also define your own budget categories and add them to some or all of the budgets you create. "Rent" is an example of an expense category. "Salary" is a typical income category.

building code

Local regulations that control design, construction, and materials used in construction. Building codes are based on safety and health standards.

buydown account

An account in which funds are held so that they can be applied as part of the monthly mortgage payment as each payment comes due during the period that an interest rate buydown plan is in effect.

buydown mortgage

A temporary buydown is a mortgage on which an initial lump sum payment is made by any party to reduce a borrower's monthly payments during the first few years of a mortgage. A permanent buydown reduces the interest rate over the entire life of a mortgage.

C

call option

A provision in the mortgage that gives the mortgagee the right to call the mortgage due and payable at the end of a specified period for whatever reason.

cap

A provision of an adjustable-rate mortgage (ARM) that limits how much the interest rate or mortgage payments may increase or decrease. See lifetime payment cap, lifetime rate cap, periodic payment cap, and periodic rate cap.

capital

(1) Money used to create income, either as an investment in a business or an income property. (2) The money or property comprising the wealth owned or used by a person or business enterprise. (3) The accumulated wealth of a person or busi-

ness. (4) The net worth of a business represented by the amount by which its assets exceed liabilities.

capital expenditure

The cost of an improvement made to extend the useful life of a property or to add to its value.

capital improvement

Any structure or component erected as a permanent improvement to real property that adds to its value and useful life.

cash-out refinance

A refinance transaction in which the amount of money received from the new loan exceeds the total of the money needed to repay the existing first mortgage, closing costs, points, and the amount required to satisfy any outstanding subordinate mortgage liens. In other words, a refinance transaction in which the borrower receives additional cash that can be used for any purpose.

certificate of deposit

A document written by a bank or other financial institution that is evidence of a deposit, with the issuer's promise to return the deposit plus earnings at a specified interest rate within a specified time period.

certificate of deposit index

An index that is used to determine interest rate changes for certain ARM plans. It represents the weekly average of secondary market interest rates on six-month negotiable certificates of deposit. See adjustable-rate mortgage (ARM).

Certificate of Eligibility

A document issued by the federal government certifying a veteran's eligibility for a Department of Veterans Affairs (VA) mortgage.

Certificate of Reasonable Value (CRV)

A document issued by the Department of Veterans Affairs (VA) that establishes the maximum value and loan amount for a VA mortgage.

certificate of title

A statement provided by an abstract company, title company, or attorney stating that the title to real estate is legally held by the current owner.

chain of title

The history of all of the documents that transfer title to a parcel of real property, starting with the earliest existing document and ending with the most recent.

change frequency

The frequency (in months) of payment and/or interest rate changes in an adjustable-rate mortgage (ARM).

chattel

Another name for personal property.

clear title

A title that is free of liens or legal questions as to ownership of the property.

closing

A meeting at which a sale of a property is finalized by the buyer signing the mortgage documents and paying closing costs. Also called "settlement."

closing cost item

A fee or amount that a home buyer must pay at closing for a single service, tax, or product. Closing costs are made up of individual closing cost items such as origination fees and attorney's fees. Many closing cost items are included as numbered items on the HUD-1 statement.

closing costs

Expenses (over and above the price of the property) incurred by buyers and sellers in transferring ownership of a property. Closing costs normally include an origination fee, an attorney's fee, taxes, an amount placed in escrow, and charges for obtaining title insurance and a survey. Closing costs percentage will vary according to the area of the country; lenders or Realtors® often provide estimates of closing costs to prospective homebuyers.

closing statement

See HUD-1 statement.

cloud on title

Any conditions revealed by a title search that adversely affect the title to real estate. Usually clouds on title cannot be removed except by a quitclaim deed, release, or court action.

coinsurance

A sharing of insurance risk between the insurer and the insured. Coinsurance depends on the relationship between the amount of the policy and a specified percentage of the actual value of the property insured at the time of the loss.

coinsurance clause

A provision in a hazard insurance policy that states the amount of coverage that must be maintained — as a percentage of the total value of the property — for the insured to collect the full amount of a loss.

collateral

An asset (such as a car or a home) that guarantees the repayment of a loan. The borrower risks losing the asset if the loan is not repaid according to the terms of the loan contract.

collection

The efforts used to bring a delinquent mortgage current and to file the necessary notices to proceed with foreclosure when necessary.

co-maker

A person who signs a promissory note along with the borrower. A co-maker's signature guarantees that the loan will be repaid, because the borrower and the co-maker are equally responsible for the repayment. See endorser.

commission

The fee charged by a broker or agent for negotiating a real estate or loan transaction. A commission is generally a percentage of the price of the property or loan.

commitment letter

A formal offer by a lender stating the terms under which it agrees to lend money to a home buyer. Also known as a "loan commitment."

common area assessments

Levies against individual unit owners in a condominium or planned unit development (PUD) project for additional capital to defray homeowners' association costs and expenses and to repair, replace, maintain, improve, or operate the common areas of the project.

common areas

Those portions of a building, land, and amenities owned (or managed) by a planned unit development (PUD) or condominium project's homeowners' association (or a cooperative project's cooperative corporation) that are used by all of the unit owners, who share in the common expenses of their operation and maintenance. Common areas include swimming pools, tennis courts, and other recreational facilities, as well as common corridors of buildings, parking areas, means of ingress and egress, etc.

common law

An unwritten body of law based on general custom in England

and used to an extent in the United States.

Community Home Improvement Mortgage Loan®
An alternative financing option that allows low- and moderate-income home buyers to obtain 95 percent financing for the purchase and improvement of a home in need of modest repairs. The repair work can account for as much as 30 percent of the appraised value.

Community Land Trust Mortgage Loan
An alternative financing option that enables low- and moderate-income home buyers to purchase housing that has been improved by a nonprofit Community Land Trust and to lease the land on which the property stands.

community property
In some western and southwestern states, a form of ownership under which property acquired during a marriage is presumed to be owned jointly unless acquired as separate property of either spouse.

Community Seconds®
An alternative financing option for low- and moderate-income households under which an investor purchases a first mortgage that has a subsidized second mortgage behind it. The second mortgage may be issued by a state, county, or local housing agency, foundation, or nonprofit organization. Payment on the second mortgage is often deferred and carries a very low interest rate (or no interest rate at all). Part of the debt may be forgiven incrementally for each year the buyer remains in the home.

comparables

An abbreviation for "comparable properties"; used for comparative purposes in the appraisal process. Comparables are properties like the property under consideration; they have reasonably the same size, location , and amenities and have recently been sold. Comparables help the appraiser determine the approximate fair market value of the subject property.

compound interest

Interest paid on the original principal balance and on the accrued and unpaid interest.

condemnation

The determination that a building is not fit for use or is dangerous and must be destroyed; the taking of private property for a public purpose through an exercise of the right of eminent domain.

condominium

A real estate project in which each unit owner has title to a unit in a building, an undivided interest in the common areas of the project, and sometimes the exclusive use of certain limited common areas.

condominium conversion

Changing the ownership of an existing building (usually a rental project) to the condominium form of ownership.

condominium hotel

A condominium project that has rental or registration desks,

short-term occupancy, food and telephone services, and daily cleaning services and that is operated as a commercial hotel even though the units are individually owned.

construction loan

A short-term, interim loan for financing the cost of construction. The lender makes payments to the builder at periodic intervals as the work progresses.

consumer reporting agency (or bureau)

An organization that prepares reports that are used by lenders to determine a potential borrower's credit history. The agency obtains data for these reports from a credit repository as well as from other sources.

contingency

A condition that must be met before a contract is legally binding. For example, home purchasers often include a contingency that specifies that the contract is not binding until the purchaser obtains a satisfactory home inspection report from a qualified home inspector.

contract

An oral or written agreement to do or not to do a certain thing.

conventional mortgage

A mortgage that is not insured or guaranteed by the federal government. Contrast with government mortgage.

convertibility clause

A provision in some adjustable-rate mortgages (ARMs) that

allows the borrower to change the ARM to a fixed-rate mortgage at specified timeframes after loan origination.

convertible ARM
An adjustable-rate mortgage (ARM) that can be converted to a fixed-rate mortgage under specified conditions.

cooperative (co-op)
A type of multiple ownership in which the residents of a multi-unit housing complex own shares in the cooperative corporation that owns the property, giving each resident the right to occupy a specific apartment or unit.

cooperative corporation
A business trust entity that holds title to a cooperative project and grants occupancy rights to particular apartments or units to shareholders through proprietary leases or similar arrangements.

cooperative mortgages
Mortgages related to a cooperative project. This usually refers to the multifamily mortgage covering the entire project but occasionally describes the share loans on the individual units.

cooperative project
A residential or mixed-use building wherein a corporation or trust holds title to the property and sells shares of stock representing the value of a single apartment unit to individuals who, in turn, receive a proprietary lease as evidence of title.

corporate relocation
Arrangements under which an employer moves an employee

to another area as part of the employer's normal course of business or under which it transfers a substantial part or all of its operations and employees to another area because it is relocating its headquarters or expanding its office capacity.

cost of funds index (COFI)

An index that is used to determine interest rate changes for certain adjustable-rate mortgage (ARM) plans. It represents the weighted-average cost of savings, borrowings, and advances of the 11th District members of the Federal Home Loan Bank of San Francisco. See adjustable-rate mortgage (ARM).

covenant

A clause in a mortgage that obligates or restricts the borrower and that, if violated, can result in foreclosure.

credit

An agreement in which a borrower receives something of value in exchange for a promise to repay the lender at a later date.

credit history

A record of an individual's open and fully repaid debts. A credit history helps a lender to determine whether a potential borrower has a history of repaying debts in a timely manner.

credit life insurance

A type of insurance often bought by mortgagors because it will pay off the mortgage debt if the mortgagor dies while the policy is in force.

creditor

A person to whom money is owed.

credit report

A report of an individual's credit history prepared by a credit bureau and used by a lender in determining a loan applicant's creditworthiness. See merged credit report.

credit repository

An organization that gathers, records, updates, and stores financial and public records information about the payment records of individuals who are being considered for credit.

D

debt

An amount owed to another. See installment loan and revolving liability.

deed

The legal document conveying title to a property.

deed-in-lieu

A deed given by a mortgagor to the mortgagee to satisfy a debt and avoid foreclosure. Also called a "voluntary conveyance."

deed of trust

The document used in some states instead of a mortgage; title is conveyed to a trustee.

default

Failure to make mortgage payments on a timely basis or to comply with other requirements of a mortgage.

delinquency

Failure to make mortgage payments when mortgage payments are due.

deposit

A sum of money given to bind the sale of real estate, or a sum of money given to ensure payment or an advance of funds in the processing of a loan. See earnest money deposit.

depreciation

A decline in the value of property; the opposite of appreciation.

discount points

See point.

dower

The rights of a widow in the property of her husband at his death.

down payment

The part of the purchase price of a property that the buyer pays in cash and does not finance with a mortgage.

due-on-sale provision

A provision in a mortgage that allows the lender to demand repayment in full if the borrower sells the property that serves as security for the mortgage.

due-on-transfer provision

This terminology is usually used for second mortgages. See due-on-sale provision.

E

earnest money deposit

A deposit made by the potential home buyer to show that he or she is serious about buying the house.

easement

A right of way giving persons other than the owner access to or over a property.

effective age

An appraiser's estimate of the physical condition of a building. The actual age of a building may be shorter or longer than its effective age.

effective gross income

Normal annual income including overtime that is regular or guaranteed. The income may be from more than one source. Salary is generally the principal source, but other income may qualify if it is significant and stable.

eminent domain

The right of a government to take private property for public use upon payment of its fair market value. Eminent domain is the basis for condemnation proceedings.

Employer-assisted housing

A special Fannie Mae housing initiative that offers several different ways for employers to work with local lenders to develop plans to assist their employees in purchasing homes.

encroachment

An improvement that intrudes illegally on another's property.

encumbrance

Anything that affects or limits the fee simple title to a property, such as mortgages, leases, easements, or restrictions.

Endorser

A person who signs ownership interest over to another party. Contrast with co-maker.

Equal Credit Opportunity Act (ECOA)

A federal law that requires lenders and other creditors to make credit equally available without discrimination based on race, color, religion, national origin, age, sex, marital status, or receipt of income from public assistance programs.

equity

A homeowner's financial interest in a property. Equity is the difference between the fair market value of the property and the amount still owed on its mortgage.

escrow

An item of value, money, or documents deposited with a third party to be delivered upon the fulfillment of a condition. For example, the deposit by a borrower with the lender of funds to pay taxes and insurance premiums when they become due, or the deposit of funds or documents with an attorney or escrow agent to be disbursed upon the closing of a sale of real estate.

escrow account
The account in which a mortgage servicer holds the borrower's escrow payments prior to paying property expenses.

escrow analysis
The periodic examination of escrow accounts to determine if current monthly deposits will provide sufficient funds to pay taxes, insurance, and other bills when due.

escrow collections
Funds collected by the servicer and set aside in an escrow account to pay the borrower's property taxes, mortgage insurance, and hazard insurance.

escrow disbursements
The use of escrow funds to pay real estate taxes, hazard insurance, mortgage insurance, and other property expenses as they become due.

escrow payment
The portion of a mortgagor's monthly payment that is held by the servicer to pay for taxes, hazard insurance, mortgage insurance, lease payments, and other items as they become due. Known as "impounds" or "reserves" in some states.

estate

The ownership interest of an individual in real property. The sum total of all the real property and personal property owned by an individual at time of death.

eviction

The lawful expulsion of an occupant from real property.

examination of title

The report on the title of a property from the public records or an abstract of the title.

exclusive listing

A written contract that gives a licensed real estate agent the exclusive right to sell a property for a specified time, but reserving the owner's right to sell the property alone without the payment of a commission.

executor

A person named in a will to administer an estate. The court will appoint an administrator if no executor is named. "Executrix" is the feminine form.

F

Fair Credit Reporting Act

A consumer protection law that regulates the disclosure of consumer credit reports by consumer/credit reporting agencies and establishes procedures for correcting mistakes on one's credit record.

fair market value

The highest price that a buyer, willing but not compelled to buy, would pay, and the lowest a seller, willing but not compelled to sell, would accept.

Fannie Mae

A New York Stock Exchange company and the largest non-bank financial services company in the world. It operates pursuant to a federal charter and is the nation's largest source of financing for home mortgages. Over the past 30 years, Fannie Mae has provided nearly $2.5 trillion of mortgage financing for over 30 million families.

Fannie Mae's Community Home Buyer's Program℠

An income-based community lending model, under which mortgage insurers and Fannie Mae offer flexible underwriting guidelines to increase a low- or moderate-income family's buying power and to decrease the total amount of cash needed to purchase a home. Borrowers who participate in this model are required to attend pre-purchase home-buyer education sessions.

Fannie 97®

A financing option for a fixed-rate mortgage that offers home buyers a 3 percent down payment loan with either a 25- or 30-year term. The mortgage features a loan-to-value (LTV) percentage of 97 percent, and is designed to expand home-ownership opportunities for people with modest incomes. Borrowers must take a pre-purchase home-buyer education session to qualify for a Fannie 97 mortgage.

Federal Housing Administration (FHA)
An agency of the U.S. Department of Housing and Urban Development (HUD). Its main activity is the insuring of residential mortgage loans made by private lenders. The FHA sets standards for construction and underwriting but does not lend money or plan or construct housing.

fee simple
The greatest possible interest a person can have in real estate.

fee simple estate
An unconditional, unlimited estate of inheritance that represents the greatest estate and most extensive interest in land that can be enjoyed. It is of perpetual duration. When the real estate is in a condominium project, the unit owner is the exclusive owner only of the air space within his or her portion of the building (the unit) and is an owner in common with respect to the land and other common portions of the property.

FHA coinsured mortgage
A mortgage (under FHA Section 244) for which the Federal Housing Administration (FHA) and the originating lender share the risk of loss in the event of the mortgagor's default.

FHA mortgage
A mortgage that is insured by the Federal Housing Administration (FHA). Also known as a government mortgage.

finder's fee
A fee or commission paid to a mortgage broker for finding a mortgage loan for a prospective borrower.

firm commitment

A lender's agreement to make a loan to a specific borrower on a specific property.

first mortgage

A mortgage that is the primary lien against a property.

fixed installment

The monthly payment due on a mortgage loan. The fixed installment includes payment of both principal and interest.

fixed-rate mortgage (FRM)

A mortgage in which the interest rate does not change during the entire term of the loan.

fixture

Personal property that becomes real property when attached in a permanent manner to real estate.

flood insurance

Insurance that compensates for physical property damage resulting from flooding. It is required for properties located in federally designated flood areas.

foreclosure

The legal process by which a borrower in default under a mortgage is deprived of his or her interest in the mortgaged property. This usually involves a forced sale of the property at public auction with the proceeds of the sale being applied to the mortgage debt.

forfeiture
The loss of money, property, rights, or privileges due to a breach of legal obligation.

401(k)/403(b)
An employer-sponsored investment plan that allows individuals to set aside tax-deferred income for retirement or emergency purposes. 401(k) plans are provided by employers that are private corporations. 403(b) plans are provided by employers that are not for profit organizations.

401(k)/403(b) loan
Some administrators of 401(k)/403(b) plans allow for loans against the monies you have accumulated in these plans — monies must be repaid to avoid serious penalty charges.

fully amortized ARM
An adjustable-rate mortgage (ARM) with a monthly payment that is sufficient to amortize the remaining balance, at the interest accrual rate, over the amortization term.

government mortgage
A mortgage that is insured by the Federal Housing Administration (FHA) or guaranteed by the Department of Veterans Affairs (VA) or the Rural Housing Service (RHS). Contrast with conventional mortgage.

Government National Mortgage Association
A government-owned corporation within the U.S. Department

of Housing and Urban Development (HUD). Created by Congress on September 1, 1968, GNMA assumed responsibility for the special assistance loan program formerly administered by Fannie Mae. Popularly known as Ginnie Mae.

grantee
The person to whom an interest in real property is conveyed.

grantor
The person conveying an interest in real property.

ground rent
The amount of money that is paid for the use of land when title to a property is held as a leasehold estate rather than as a fee simple estate.

group home
A single-family residential structure designed or adapted for occupancy by unrelated developmentally disabled persons. The structure provides long-term housing and support services that are residential in nature.

growing-equity mortgage (GEM)
A fixed-rate mortgage that provides scheduled payment increases over an established period of time, with the increased amount of the monthly payment applied directly toward reducing the remaining balance of the mortgage.

guarantee mortgage
A mortgage that is guaranteed by a third party.

guaranteed loan

Also known as a government mortgage.

H

hazard insurance

Insurance coverage that compensates for physical damage to a property from fire, wind, vandalism, or other hazards.

Home Equity Conversion Mortgage (HECM)

A special type of mortgage that enables older home owners to convert the equity they have in their homes into cash, using a variety of payment options to address their specific financial needs. Unlike traditional home equity loans, a borrower does not qualify on the basis of income but on the value of his or her home. In addition, the loan does not have to be repaid until the borrower no longer occupies the property. Sometimes called a reverse mortgage.

home equity line of credit

A mortgage loan, which is usually in a subordinate position, that allows the borrower to obtain multiple advances of the loan proceeds at his or her own discretion, up to an amount that represents a specified percentage of the borrower's equity in a property.

home inspection

A thorough inspection that evaluates the structural and

mechanical condition of a property. A satisfactory home inspection is often included as a contingency by the purchaser. Contrast with appraisal.

HomeKeeper℠

Fannie Mae's adjustable-rate conventional reverse mortgage, which allows older homeowners to borrow against the value of their homes and receive the proceeds according to the payment option they select. The amount available is based on the number of borrowers and their ages and the adjusted property value. Anyone 62 years or older who either owns his or her own home free and clear or has very low mortgage debt is eligible.

homeowners' association

A nonprofit association that manages the common areas of a planned unit development (PUD) or condominium project. In a condominium project, it has no ownership interest in the common elements. In a PUD project, it holds title to the common elements.

homeowner's insurance

An insurance policy that combines personal liability insurance and hazard insurance coverage for a dwelling and its contents.

homeowner's warranty (HOW)

A type of insurance that covers repairs to specified parts of a house for a specific period of time. It is provided by the builder or property seller as a condition of the sale.

HomeStyle® Mortgage Loan

A mortgage that enables eligible borrowers to obtain financing to remodel, repair, and upgrade their existing homes or homes that they are purchasing. The financing takes the form of a conventional second mortgage or a Federal Housing Administration (FHA) Section 203(k) first mortgage.

housing expense ratio

The percentage of gross monthly income that goes toward paying housing expenses.

HUD median income

Median family income for a particular county or metropolitan statistical area (MSA), as estimated by the Department of Housing and Urban Development (HUD).

HUD-1 statement

A document that provides an itemized listing of the funds that are payable at closing. Items that appear on the statement include real estate commissions, loan fees, points, and initial escrow amounts. Each item on the statement is represented by a separate number within a standardized numbering system. The totals at the bottom of the HUD-1 statement define the seller's net proceeds and the buyer's net payment at closing. The blank form for the statement is published by the Department of Housing and Urban Development (HUD). The HUD-1 statement is also known as the "closing statement" or "settlement sheet."

I

income property

Real estate developed or improved to produce income.

index

A number used to compute the interest rate for an adjustable-rate mortgage (ARM). The index is generally a published number or percentage, such as the average interest rate or yield on Treasury bills. A margin is added to the index to determine the interest rate that will be charged on the ARM. This interest rate is subject to any caps that are associated with the mortgage.

in-file credit report

An objective account, normally computer-generated, of credit and legal information obtained from a credit repository.

inflation

An increase in the amount of money or credit available in relation to the amount of goods or services available, which causes an increase in the general price level of goods and services. Over time, inflation reduces the purchasing power of a dollar, making it worth less.

initial interest rate

The original interest rate of the mortgage at the time of closing. This rate changes for an adjustable-rate mortgage (ARM). Sometimes known as "start rate" or "teaser."

installment

The regular periodic payment that a borrower agrees to make to a lender.

installment loan

Borrowed money that is repaid in equal payments, known as installments. A furniture loan is often paid for as an installment loan.

insurable title

A property title that a title insurance company agrees to insure against defects and disputes.

insurance

A contract that provides compensation for specific losses in exchange for a periodic payment. An individual contract is known as an insurance policy, and the periodic payment is known as an insurance premium.

insurance binder

A document that states that insurance is temporarily in effect. Because the coverage will expire by a specified date, a permanent policy must be obtained before the expiration date.

insured mortgage

A mortgage that is protected by the Federal Housing Administration (FHA) or by private mortgage insurance (MI). If the borrower defaults on the loan, the insurer must pay the lender the lesser of the loss incurred or the insured amount.

interest

The fee charged for borrowing money.

interest accrual rate

The percentage rate at which interest accrues on the mortgage. In most cases, it is also the rate used to calculate the monthly payments, although it is not used for an adjustable-rate mortgage (ARM) with payment change limitations.

interest rate

The rate of interest in effect for the monthly payment due.

interest rate buydown plan

An arrangement wherein the property seller (or any other party) deposits money to an account so that it can be released each month to reduce the mortgagor's monthly payments during the early years of a mortgage. During the specified period, the mortgagor's effective interest rate is "bought down" below the actual interest rate.

interest rate ceiling

For an adjustable-rate mortgage (ARM), the maximum interest rate, as specified in the mortgage note.

interest rate floor

For an adjustable-rate mortgage (ARM), the minimum interest rate, as specified in the mortgage note.

investment property

A property that is not occupied by the owner.

IRA (Individual Retirement Account)
A retirement account that allows individuals to make tax-deferred contributions to a personal retirement fund. Individuals can place IRA funds in bank accounts or in other forms of investment such as stocks, bonds, or mutual funds.

J

joint tenancy
A form of co-ownership that gives each tenant equal interest and equal rights in the property, including the right of survivorship.

judgment
A decision made by a court of law. In judgments that require the repayment of a debt, the court may place a lien against the debtor's real property as collateral for the judgment's creditor.

judgment lien
A lien on the property of a debtor resulting from the decree of a court.

judicial foreclosure
A type of foreclosure proceeding used in some states that is handled as a civil lawsuit and conducted entirely under the auspices of a court.

jumbo loan
A loan that exceeds Fannie Mae's legislated mortgage amount limits. Also called a nonconforming loan.

L

late charge

The penalty a borrower must pay when a payment is made a stated number of days (usually 15) after the due date.

lease

A written agreement between the property owner and a tenant that stipulates the conditions under which the tenant may possess the real estate for a specified period of time and rent.

leasehold estate

A way of holding title to a property wherein the mortgagor does not actually own the property but rather has a recorded long-term lease on it.

lease-purchase mortgage loan

An alternative financing option that allows low- and moderate-income home buyers to lease a home from a nonprofit organization with an option to buy. Each month's rent payment consists of principal, interest, taxes and insurance (PITI) payments on the first mortgage plus an extra amount that is earmarked for deposit to a savings account in which money for a downpayment will accumulate.

legal description

A property description, recognized by law, that is sufficient to locate and identify the property without oral testimony.

liabilities

A person's financial obligations. Liabilities include long-term and short-term debt, as well as any other amounts that are owed to others.

liability insurance

Insurance coverage that offers protection against claims alleging that a property owner's negligence or inappropriate action resulted in bodily injury or property damage to another party.

lien

A legal claim against a property that must be paid off when the property is sold.

lifetime payment cap

For an adjustable-rate mortgage (ARM), a limit on the amount that payments can increase or decrease over the life of the mortgage. See cap.

lifetime rate cap

For an adjustable-rate mortgage (ARM), a limit on the amount that the interest rate can increase or decrease over the life of the loan. See cap.

line of credit

An agreement by a commercial bank or other financial institution to extend credit up to a certain amount for a certain time to a specified borrower. See home equity line of credit.

liquid asset

A cash asset or an asset that is easily converted into cash.

loan

A sum of borrowed money (principal) that is generally repaid with interest.

loan commitment

See commitment letter.

loan origination

The process by which a mortgage lender brings into existence a mortgage secured by real property.

loan-to-value (LTV) percentage

The relationship between the principal balance of the mortgage and the appraised value (or sales price if it is lower) of the property. For example, a $100,000 home with an $80,000 mortgage has a LTV percentage of 80 percent.

lock-in

A written agreement in which the lender guarantees a specified interest rate if a mortgage goes to closing within a set period of time. The lock-in also usually specifies the number of points to be paid at closing.

lock-in period

The time period during which the lender has guaranteed an interest rate to a borrower. See lock-in.

M

margin

For an adjustable-rate mortgage (ARM), the amount that is added to the index to establish the interest rate on each adjustment date, subject to any limitations on the interest rate change.

master association

A homeowners' association in a large condominium or planned unit development (PUD) project that is made up of representatives from associations covering specific areas within the project. In effect, it is a "second-level" association that handles matters affecting the entire development, while the "first-level" associations handle matters affecting their particular portions of the project.

maturity

The date on which the principal balance of a loan, bond, or other financial instrument becomes due and payable.

maximum financing

A mortgage amount that is within 5 percent of the highest loan-to-value (LTV) percentage allowed for a specific product. Thus, maximum financing on a fixed-rate mortgage would be 90 percent or higher, because 95 percent is the maximum allowable LTV percentage for that product.

merged credit report

A credit report that contains information from three credit

repositories. When the report is created, the information is compared for duplicate entries. Any duplicates are combined to provide a summary of a your credit.

modification

The act of changing any of the terms of the mortgage.

money market account

A savings account that provides bank depositors with many of the advantages of a money market fund. Certain regulatory restrictions apply to the withdrawal of funds from a money market account.

money market fund

A mutual fund that allows individuals to participate in managed investments in short-term debt securities, such as certificates of deposit and Treasury bills.

monthly fixed installment

That portion of the total monthly payment that is applied toward principal and interest. When a mortgage negatively amortizes, the monthly fixed installment does not include any amount for principal reduction.

monthly payment mortgage

A mortgage that requires payments to reduce the debt once a month.

mortgage

A legal document that pledges a property to the lender as

security for payment of a debt.

mortgage banker

A company that originates mortgages exclusively for resale in the secondary mortgage market.

mortgage broker

An individual or company that brings borrowers and lenders together for the purpose of loan origination. Mortgage brokers typically require a fee or a commission for their services.

mortgagee

The lender in a mortgage agreement.

mortgage insurance

A contract that insures the lender against loss caused by a mortgagor's default on a government mortgage or conventional mortgage. Mortgage insurance can be issued by a private company or by a government agency such as the Federal Housing Administration (FHA). Depending on the type of mortgage insurance, the insurance may cover a percentage of or virtually all of the mortgage loan. See private mortgage insurance (MI).

mortgage insurance premium (MIP)

The amount paid by a mortgagor for mortgage insurance, either to a government agency such as the Federal Housing Administration (FHA) or to a private mortgage insurance (MI) company.

mortgage life insurance

A type of term life insurance often bought by mortgagors. The amount of coverage decreases as the principal balance declines. In the event that the borrower dies while the policy is in force, the debt is automatically satisfied by insurance proceeds.

mortgagor

The borrower in a mortgage agreement.

multidwelling units

Properties that provide separate housing units for more than one family, although they secure only a single mortgage.

multifamily mortgage

A residential mortgage on a dwelling that is designed to house more than four families, such as a high-rise apartment complex.

N

negative amortization

A gradual increase in mortgage debt that occurs when the monthly payment is not large enough to cover the entire principal and interest due. The amount of the shortfall is added to the remaining balance to create "negative" amortization.

net cash flow

The income that remains for an investment property after the monthly operating income is reduced by the monthly housing expense, which includes principal, interest, taxes, and insurance (PITI) for the mortgage, homeowners' association dues, leasehold payments, and subordinate financing payments.

net worth
The value of all of a person's assets, including cash, minus all liabilities.

no cash-out refinance
A refinance transaction in which the new mortgage amount is limited to the sum of the remaining balance of the existing first mortgage, closing costs (including prepaid items), points, the amount required to satisfy any mortgage liens that are more than one year old (if the borrower chooses to satisfy them), and other funds for the borrower's use (as long as the amount does not exceed 1 percent of the principal amount of the new mortgage).

nonliquid asset
An asset that cannot easily be converted into cash.

note
A legal document that obligates a borrower to repay a mortgage loan at a stated interest rate during a specified period of time.

note rate
The interest rate stated on a mortgage note.

notice of default
A formal written notice to a borrower that a default has

occurred and that legal action may be taken.

original principal balance
The total amount of principal owed on a mortgage before any payments are made.

origination fee
A fee paid to a lender for processing a loan application. The origination fee is stated in the form of points. One point is 1 percent of the mortgage amount.

owner financing
A property purchase transaction in which the property seller provides all or part of the financing.

P

partial payment
A payment that is not sufficient to cover the scheduled monthly payment on a mortgage loan.

payment change date
The date when a new monthly payment amount takes effect on an adjustable-rate mortgage (ARM) or a graduated-payment adjustable-rate mortgage (GPARM). Generally, the payment change date occurs in the month immediately after the adjustment date.

periodic payment cap

For an adjustable-rate mortgage (ARM), a limit on the amount that payments can increase or decrease during any one adjustment period. See cap.

periodic rate cap

For an adjustable-rate mortgage (ARM), a limit on the amount that the interest rate can increase or decrease during any one adjustment period, regardless of how high or low the index might be. See cap.

personal property

Any property that is not real property.

PITI

See principal, interest, taxes, and insurance (PITI).

PITI reserves

A cash amount that a borrower must have on hand after making a down payment and paying all closing costs for the purchase of a home. The principal, interest, taxes, and insurance (PITI) reserves must equal the amount that the borrower would have to pay for PITI for a predefined number of months.

planned unit development

See PUD.

point

A one-time charge by the lender for originating a loan. A point is 1 percent of the amount of the mortgage.

power of attorney

A legal document that authorizes another person to act on one's behalf. A power of attorney can grant complete authority or can be limited to certain acts and/or certain periods of time.

prearranged refinancing agreement

A formal or informal arrangement between a lender and a borrower wherein the lender agrees to offer special terms (such as a reduction in the costs) for a future refinancing of a mortgage being originated as an inducement for the borrower to enter into the original mortgage transaction.

preforeclosure sale

A procedure in which the investor allows a mortgagor to avoid foreclosure by selling the property for less than the amount that is owed to the investor.

prepayment

Any amount paid to reduce the principal balance of a loan before the due date. Payment in full on a mortgage that may result from a sale of the property, the owner's decision to pay off the loan in full, or a foreclosure. In each case, prepayment means payment occurs before the loan has been fully amortized.

prepayment penalty

A fee that may be charged to a borrower who pays off a loan before it is due.

pre-qualification

The process of determining how much money a prospective home buyer will be eligible to borrow before he or she applies for a loan.

prime rate

The interest rate that banks charge to their preferred customers. Changes in the prime rate influence changes in other rates, including mortgage interest rates.

principal

The amount borrowed or remaining unpaid. The part of the monthly payment that reduces the remaining balance of a mortgage.

principal balance

The outstanding balance of principal on a mortgage. The principal balance does not include interest or any other charges. See remaining balance.

principal, interest, taxes, and insurance (PITI)

The four components of a monthly mortgage payment. Principal refers to the part of the monthly payment that reduces the remaining balance of the mortgage. Interest is the fee charged for borrowing money. Taxes and insurance refer to the amounts that are paid into an escrow account each month for property taxes and mortgage and hazard insurance.

private mortgage insurance (MI)

Mortgage insurance that is provided by a private mortgage

insurance company to protect lenders against loss if a borrower defaults. Most lenders generally require MI for a loan with a loan-to-value (LTV) percentage in excess of 80 percent.

promissory note

A written promise to repay a specified amount over a specified period of time.

public auction

A meeting in an announced public location to sell property to repay a mortgage that is in default.

Planned Unit Development (PUD)

A project or subdivision that includes common property that is owned and maintained by a homeowners' association for the benefit and use of the individual PUD unit owners.

purchase and sale agreement

A written contract signed by the buyer and seller stating the terms and conditions under which a property will be sold.

purchase money transaction

The acquisition of property through the payment of money or its equivalent.

Q

qualifying ratios

Calculations that are used in determining whether a borrower can qualify for a mortgage. They consist of two separate calculations:

a housing expense as a percent of income ratio and total debt obligations as a percent of income ratio.

quitclaim deed

A deed that transfers without warranty whatever interest or title a grantor may have at the time the conveyance is made.

R

radon

A radioactive gas found in some homes that in sufficient concentrations can cause health problems.

rate-improvement mortgage

A fixed-rate mortgage that includes a provision that gives the borrower a one-time option to reduce the interest rate (without refinancing) during the early years of the mortgage term.

rate lock

A commitment issued by a lender to a borrower or other mortgage originator guaranteeing a specified interest rate for a specified period of time. See lock-in.

real estate agent

A person licensed to negotiate and transact the sale of real estate on behalf of the property owner.

Real Estate Settlement Procedures Act (RESPA)

A consumer protection law that requires lenders to give borrowers advance notice of closing costs.

real property

Land and appurtenances, including anything of a permanent nature such as structures, trees, minerals, and the interest, benefits, and inherent rights thereof.

Realtor®

A real estate broker or an associate who holds active membership in a local real estate board that is affiliated with the National Association of Realtors®.

recission

The cancellation or annulment of a transaction or contract by the operation of a law or by mutual consent. Borrowers usually have the option to cancel a refinance transaction within three business days after it has closed.

recorder

The public official who keeps records of transactions that affect real property in the area. Sometimes known as a "Registrar of Deeds" or "County Clerk."

recording

The noting in the registrar's office of the details of a properly executed legal document, such as a deed, a mortgage note, a satisfaction of mortgage, or an extension of mortgage, thereby making it a part of the public record.

refinance transaction

The process of paying off one loan with the proceeds from a new loan using the same property as security.

rehabilitation mortgage

A mortgage created to cover the costs of repairing, improving, and sometimes acquiring an existing property.

remaining balance

The amount of principal that has not yet been repaid. See principal balance.

remaining term

The original amortization term minus the number of payments that have been applied.

rent loss insurance

Insurance that protects a landlord against loss of rent or rental value due to fire or other casualty that renders the leased premises unavailable for use and as a result of which the tenant is excused from paying rent.

rent with option to buy

See lease-purchase mortgage loan.

repayment plan

An arrangement made to repay delinquent installments or advances. Lenders' formal repayment plans are called "relief provisions."

replacement reserve fund

A fund set aside for replacement of common property in a condominium, PUD, or cooperative project — particularly that which has a short life expectancy, such as carpeting, furniture, etc.

revolving liability

A credit arrangement, such as a credit card, that allows a customer to borrow against a preapproved line of credit when purchasing goods and services. The borrower is billed for the amount that is actually borrowed plus any interest due.

right of first refusal
A provision in an agreement that requires the owner of a property to give another party the first opportunity to purchase or lease the property before he or she offers it for sale or lease to others.

right of ingress or egress
The right to enter or leave designated premises.

right of survivorship
In joint tenancy, the right of survivors to acquire the interest of a deceased joint tenant.

Rural Housing Service (RHS)
An agency within the Department of Agriculture, which operates principally under the Consolidated Farm and Rural Development Act of 1921 and Title V of the Housing Act of 1949. This agency provides financing to farmers and other qualified borrowers buying property in rural areas who are unable to obtain loans elsewhere. Funds are borrowed from the U.S. Treasury.

S

sale-leaseback
A technique in which a seller deeds property to a buyer for a consideration, and the buyer simultaneously leases the property back to the seller.

second mortgage

A mortgage that has a lien position subordinate to the first mortgage.

secondary mortgage market

The buying and selling of existing mortgages.

secured loan

A loan that is backed by collateral.

security

The property that will be pledged as collateral for a loan.

seller take-back

An agreement in which the owner of a property provides financing, often in combination with an assumable mortgage. See owner financing.

servicer

An organization that collects principal and interest payments from borrowers and manages borrowers' escrow accounts. The servicer often services mortgages that have been purchased by an investor in the secondary mortgage market.

servicing

The collection of mortgage payments from borrowers and related responsibilities of a loan servicer.

settlement

See closing.

settlement sheet

See HUD-1 statement.

special deposit account

An account that is established for rehabilitation mortgages to hold the funds needed for the rehabilitation work so they can be disbursed from time to time as particular portions of the work are completed.

standard payment calculation

The method used to determine the monthly payment required to repay the remaining balance of a mortgage in substantially equal installments over the remaining term of the mortgage at the current interest rate.

step-rate mortgage

A mortgage that allows for the interest rate to increase according to a specified schedule (i.e., seven years), resulting in increased payments as well. At the end of the specified period, the rate and payments will remain constant for the remainder of the loan.

subdivision

A housing development that is created by dividing a tract of land into individual lots for sale or lease.

subordinate financing

Any mortgage or other lien that has a priority that is lower than that of the first mortgage.

subsidized second mortgage

An alternative financing option known as the Community

Seconds® mortgage for low- and moderate-income households. An investor purchases a first mortgage that has a subsidized second mortgage behind it. The second mortgage may be issued by a state, county, or local housing agency, foundation, or nonprofit corporation. Payment on the second mortgage is often deferred and carries a very low interest rate (or no interest rate). Part of the debt may be forgiven incrementally for each year the buyer remains in the home.

survey

A drawing or map showing the precise legal boundaries of a property, the location of improvements, easements, rights of way, encroachments, and other physical features.

sweat equity

Contribution to the construction or rehabilitation of a property in the form of labor or services rather than cash.

T

tenancy by the entirety

A type of joint tenancy of property that provides right of survivorship and is available only to a husband and wife. Contrast with tenancy in common.

tenancy in common

A type of joint tenancy in a property without right of survivorship. Contrast with tenancy by the entirety and with joint tenacy.

tenant-stockholder

The obligee for a cooperative share loan, who is both a stockholder in a cooperative corporation and a tenant of the unit under a proprietary lease or occupancy agreement.

third-party origination

A process by which a lender uses another party to completely or partially originate, process, underwrite, close, fund, or package the mortgages it plans to deliver to the secondary mortgage market. See mortgage broker.

title

A legal document evidencing a person's right to or ownership of a property.

title company

A company that specializes in examining and insuring titles to real estate.

title insurance

Insurance that protects the lender (lender's policy) or the buyer (owner's policy) against loss arising from disputes over ownership of a property.

title search

A check of the title records to ensure that the seller is the legal owner of the property and that there are no liens or other claims outstanding.

total expense ratio

Total obligations as a percentage of gross monthly income.

The total expense ratio includes monthly housing expenses plus other monthly debts.

trade equity

Equity that results from a property purchaser giving his or her existing property (or an asset other than real estate) as trade as all or part of the down payment for the property that is being purchased.

transfer of ownership

Any means by which the ownership of a property changes hands. Lenders consider all of the following situations to be a transfer of ownership: the purchase of a property "subject to" the mortgage, the assumption of the mortgage debt by the property purchaser, and any exchange of possession of the property under a land sales contract or any other land trust device. In cases in which an inter vivos revocable trust is the borrower, lenders also consider any transfer of a beneficial interest in the trust to be a transfer of ownership.

transfer tax

State or local tax payable when title passes from one owner to another.

Treasury index

An index that is used to determine interest rate changes for certain adjustable-rate mortgage (ARM) plans. It is based on the results of auctions that the U.S. Treasury holds for its Treasury bills and securities or is derived from the U.S. Treasury's daily yield curve, which is based on the closing market bid yields on actively traded Treasury securities in the over-the-counter market. See adjustable-rate mortgage (ARM).

Truth-in-Lending

A federal law that requires lenders to fully disclose, in writing, the terms and conditions of a mortgage, including the annual percentage rate (APR) and other charges.

two-step mortgage

An adjustable-rate mortgage (ARM) that has one interest rate for the first five or seven years of its mortgage term and a different interest rate for the remainder of the amortization term.

two- to four-family property

A property that consists of a structure that provides living space (dwelling units) for two to four families, although ownership of the structure is evidenced by a single deed.

trustee

A fiduciary who holds or controls property for the benefit of another.

underwriting

The process of evaluating a loan application to determine the risk involved for the lender. Underwriting involves an analysis of the borrower's creditworthiness and the quality of the property itself.

unsecured loan

A loan that is not backed by collateral.

VA mortgage

A mortgage that is guaranteed by the Department of Veterans Affairs (VA). Also known as a government mortgage.

vested

Having the right to use a portion of a fund such as an individual retirement fund. For example, individuals who are 100 percent vested can withdraw all of the funds that are set aside for them in a retirement fund. However, taxes may be due on any funds that are actually withdrawn.

Department of Veterans Affairs (VA)

An agency of the federal government that guarantees residential mortgages made to eligible veterans of the military services. The guarantee protects the lender against loss and thus encourages lenders to make mortgages to veterans.

what-if analysis

An affordability analysis that is based on a what-if scenario. A what-if analysis is useful if you do not have complete data or if you want to explore the effect of various changes to your income, liabilities, or available funds or to the qualifying ratios or down payment expenses that are used in the analysis.

what-if scenario

A change in the amounts that is used as the basis of an affordability analysis. A what-if scenario can include changes to monthly income, debts, or down payment funds or to the qualifying ratios or down payment expenses that are used in the analysis. You can use a what-if scenario to explore different ways to improve your ability to afford a house.

wraparound mortgage

A mortgage that includes the remaining balance on an existing first mortgage plus an additional amount requested by the mortgagor. Full payments on both mortgages are made to the wraparound mortgagee, who then forwards the payments on the first mortgage to the first mortgagee.

Notes

Index

Homework Materials

These worksheets will help you find your dream home.

For your convenience, this section is detachable.
Simply tear these perforated pages out and staple
them together to make a separate booklet.

Rate the Neighborhoods

On a scale of 1 (poor) to 5 (excellent), rate the neighborhoods you are considering in the following areas...

Neighborhood	Academic Excellence of Schools	Proximity to Schools	Bus Pick-Up	Student/Teacher Ratio	Age of Neighborhood	Lot Sizes	Deed Restrictions	Convenient to Employment	Convenient to Shopping	Convenient to Hospitals	Community Amenities	**TOTAL OVERALL SCORE**

House Hunting Wish List

Save yourself some time by answering the following questions before you begin your search.

What's your price range? $ ________ to $ ________

What plan type appeals to you?
❑ One story ❑ Two story ❑ Basement

What type of exterior do you prefer?
❑ Brick ❑ Stone ❑ Siding ❑ Stucco

How many square feet do you want? ________________

How many bedrooms? _____ ❑ Master upstairs? ❑ Master downstairs?

How many bathrooms? _____

Do you need a separate space for the kids? ___

Would you use a game room? ___

Do you want a formal living room? ___

Do you want a formal dining room? ___

Would you like a large eat-in kitchen? ___

Need a home office? ___

How much storage do you want?
❑ Modest (We're not Pack Rats)
❑ Average (We still park in our garage)
❑ Lots (We love our stuff!)

What size yard would you like?
❑ Large (We enjoy yard work or we can afford to pay someone else to do it)
❑ Small (We've got better things to do)

Notes

Notes

Notes

Notes

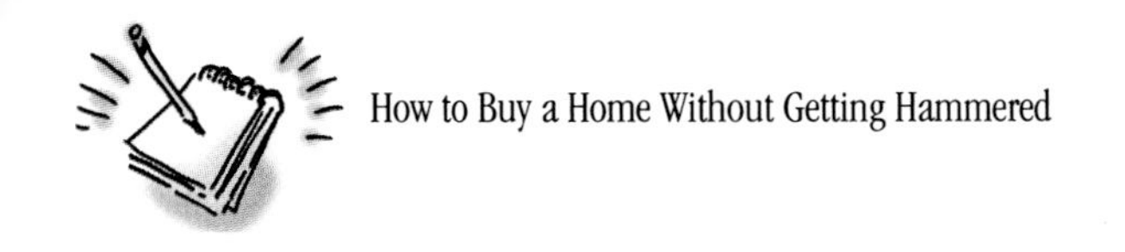

Notes

Notes

Notes

Notes

Notes

Notes